Here's what reviewers have to say about prior editions of
WHATEVER HAPPENED TO PENNY CANDY?

From the International World of Economics
Must reading for anyone who wishes to understand the basics of
our free enterprise system.   —**William E. Simon**
Former U.S. Secretary of the Treasury

This book is must reading for children of all ages. It's presentation
of some of the fundamentals of economics is lucid, accurate and
above all highly readable.
—**Michael A. Walker, Executive Director**
The Fraser Institute, British Columbia, Canada

From the World of Finance and Investment
Probably the best short course in economics around and is more
valuable than a college text that's ten times its length. Buy a dozen
and give them to friends. This is a great book!
—**Douglas Casey, Author**
Crisis Investing **and** *Strategic Investing*

Maybury's book is a valuable contribution to economic literacy. It
should be required reading for every student. Buy at least two
copies of WHATEVER HAPPENED TO PENNY CANDY: one for you and your
family; one as a gift for a member of Congress!
—**Jean Ross Peterson, Author**
It Doesn't Grow on Trees

One of the best books I've read explains the process (of government
growth and inflation) very easily — especially for people that
would like a good introduction to economics. It's also a great book
to present to your youngsters.
— **Joe Bradley**, *Investor's Hotline*

From Entrepreneurs
You'll find yourself saying "Ah...so!" more than once as you breeze through this delightful book, and you'll be looking for someone to share it with as soon as you've finished it.

— **Barbara Brabec, Editor**
National Home Business Report

Simple, easy-to-grasp explanations of such confounding economic terms as inflation, recession, velocity, and wage-price controls; combined with some fascinating glimpses into the historical economic flubs of the Romans, Germans, British, and the Americans, add up to an entertaining and informative little gem-of-a-book suitable for children and adults.   — **Jan Fletcher, former Editor**
Home Business Advisor

A refreshingly lively and comprehensive discussion of economics.
—**Ted Nicholas, Author,** *How to Form Your Own
Corporation Without a Lawyer for Under $50*

For those who feel economics is over their heads, Maybury's book brings it down to earth.   — **Busines$ Kids**

From Educators and Library Journals
Maybury's forte is explaining economics in an interesting, logical and easy-to-understand manner — no small achievement in economics pedagogy. Equally important, the economics in WHATEVER HAPPENED TO PENNY CANDY makes such good sense.   When government's economic policies make us say "uncle" let's hope it's "Uncle Eric", Maybury's letterwriter and alter ego.

— **John G. Murphy, Ph.D.**
**President of the National Schools Committee
for Economic Education, Inc.**

There is something revolutionary about the clarity of Mr. Maybury's explanations—his insight into Germany's prosperity and the method by which it was consciously achieved has the most profound implications for our own economic policy, which is also a deliberate construct. Hurray for PENNY CANDY! A brilliant book.
—**John Taylor Gatto, , author,** *Dumbing Us Down*
New York State Teacher of the Year

The quality of the writing and information presented is exceptional, and the generous use of examples gives a useful representation of economics at work in human history. (Grades 6-12)

—Educational Oasis (Good Apple)

This paperback is a concise explanation of concepts and terms taught in business education and social studies courses: money and its origin, the business cycle, inflation, recession/depression, foreign currencies, and the role of government in economics....A teacher's guide is available at a nominal fee. This book has been endorsed by educators, authors, and government officials for its unique contribution to the education of consumers from childhood to adulthood.   *—PTA Today*

An excellent introduction to economics for teens and adults that will change the way you read the paper (both the newspaper and the fine print on your dollar bills). Highly recommended.

—Mary Pride, Big Book of Home Learning

Superb introduction...This valuable little book weaves economics, history, current events, social studies, government, math and a little science into a delightfully revealing look at the foundations and workings of our monetary system. For people of any age who think economics and the business of money is beyond them and best left to the 'experts'.   *—Home Education Magazine*

For the economically illiterate, begin with the book, *Whatever Happened to Penny Candy?*, a simple, entertaining introduction to economics. *Penny Candy* introduces the economic facts of life where they touch us most — continuing increases in the cost of things. Entertaining introduction...interesting historical tidbits. Doses of economic theory....are just enough to prod thinking without overload. Excellent annotated bibliography.

—Cathy Duffy
Christian Home Educators' Curriculum Manual

Superb introduction...This valuable little book weaves economics, history, current events, social studies, government, math and a little science into a delightfully revealing look at the foundations and workings of our monetary system. For people of any age who think economics and the business of money is beyond them and best left to the 'experts'.   **—Home Education Magazine**

This little gem offers adults a basic economics education which can be used in business or personal life....inflation, price controls, and fast income operations are explored with a blend of whimsy and practicality. —*The Bookwatch*

From Authors

This one slim volume can and should replace at least one full shelf of weighty tomes. There's really no excuse for being baffled by economic theory and economic theoreticians when you can spend an evening with this grand book and learn the ABC's of a subject about which the politicians, in particular, wish you'd stay illiterate.
—**Karl Hess, Author,** *Capitalism for Kids: Growing Up to Be Your Own Boss*

And from Catalogers

This book...has come to be recognized as a refreshing and insightful explanation of economics — for students, business people and investors AND, might I add, PARENTS!... Honestly, for those of us feeling as if we are in the dark when talk rolls around to economics, it is time to move into daylight... As citizens of a country which is considered the embodiment of the free enterprise system, you owe it to yourselves and your children to understand how it all works.
—**Ann Ruethling**
Chinaberry Book Service

This book is a gem for children or adults. It explains in simple, lively terms such words as inflation, recession, velocity, wage-price controls; it shows the beauty and power of a free market, and the folly of socialistic thought....this is the best short course in economics around today.
—*Home School Horizons,* **Alpha Omega Publications**

A truly outstanding, clear, and fun explanation of free market economics based on Hayek, Mises, and Hazlitt.
—*LibertyTree Review and Catalogue*

Economics doesn't have to be stodgy, as this book proves. Letters from an economist uncle make sense out of subject many people fear. — *the Children's Small Press Collection*

Just about anyone, young or old, can read this book and immediately understand such "hard" subjects as business cycles, inflation and recession. — *the Liberator* Catalog

Quantity Discounts Available

About the "Uncle Eric" Series

The "Uncle Eric" series of books is written by Richard J. Maybury for young and old alike. Using the epistolary style of writing (using letters to tell a story), Mr. Maybury plays the part of an economist writing a series of letters to his niece or nephew. Using stories and examples, he gives interesting and clear explanations of topics that are generally thought to be too difficult for anyone but experts.

Mr. Maybury warns, "beware of anyone who tells you a topic is above you or better left to experts. Many people are twice as smart as they think they are but they've been intimidated into believing some topics are above them. You can understand almost anything if it is explained well."

The series is called UNCLE ERIC'S MODEL OF HOW THE WORLD WORKS. Each book in the series attempts to be consistent with the principles of America's Founders. The books can be read in any order, and have been written to stand alone. To get the most from each one, however, here is Mr. Maybury's suggested order of reading.

Uncle Eric's Model of How the World Works

Book 1. UNCLE ERIC TALKS ABOUT PERSONAL, CAREER AND FINANCIAL SECURITY. Uncle Eric's Model introduced.

Book 2. WHATEVER HAPPENED TO PENNY CANDY?
The economic model explained.

Book 3. WHATEVER HAPPENED TO JUSTICE?
The legal model explained. Explores America's legal heritage.

Book 4. ARE YOU LIBERAL? CONSERVATIVE? OR CONFUSED?
Political labels. What do they mean?

Book 5. ANCIENT ROME: HOW IT AFFECTS YOU TODAY.
Mr. Maybury uses historical events to explain current events.

Book 6. EVALUATING BOOKS: WHAT WOULD THOMAS JEFFERSON THINK ABOUT THIS? Learn how to identify the philosophical slant of most writers and media commentators on the subjects of law, economics, and history.

An "Uncle Eric" Book

Whatever Happened to Penny Candy?

*A fast, clear and fun explanation
of the economics you need
for success in your career,
business and investments*

By Richard J. Maybury
(Uncle Eric)

third edition
revised and expanded

Bluestocking Press
P.O. Box 1014 • Dept. PC3
Placerville, CA 95667

This is a revised edition of *Precious Metals, Politics and Paper Money: Key to Understanding Inflation and Recession* originally published by Bramble Coins, 1978

Printed in the United States of America.

Cover illustration by Bob O'Hara, Georgetown, CA
Text illustrations by Nancy Bixler
Edited by Jane A. Williams

Library of Congress Cataloging-in-Publication Data
Maybury, Rick.
    Whatever happened to penny candy? : a fast, clear, and fun
explanation of the economics you need for success in your career,
business, and investments / by Richard J. Maybury (Uncle Eric) ;
[text illustrations by Nancy Bixler]. -- 3rd ed., rev. and expanded.
        p. cm. -- (An "Uncle Eric" book)
    Includes bibliographical references.
    Summary: Explains economics as it pertains to money, inflation,
recession, and wage and price controls.
    ISBN 0-942617-15-0 : $8.95
    1. Economics, [1. Economics.]   I. Bixler, Nancy, ill.
II. Title. III. Series: Maybury, Rick. "Uncle Eric" book.
HB171.M46 1993
330.15'7--dc20   92-36378
                                                              CIP
                                                               AC

Published by   **Bluestocking Press**
                    Post Office Box 1014 • Dept. PC3
                    Placerville, CA 95667-1014

Acknowledgements

The need for this book became apparent when I was teaching Business courses to high school students. I could not find a text that explained business cycles in language students could understand, so I wrote one. Used in the classroom while under development, it was revised over and over again until it delivered the message as quickly and clearly as possible. Many thanks to the hundreds of students who offered suggestions for improvements.

Other people read this book and offered valuable comments and encouragement about it. Foremost among them was Bettina Greaves of the Foundation for Economic Education.

Over the years, I've learned a great deal about business, finance and economics, usually from reading books and articles. Harry Browne probably influenced me most, and others include Ludwig von Mises, Friedrich Hayek, Henry Hazlitt and Murray Rothbard. Mr. Hazlitt's fine little book <u>Economics in One Lesson</u> is the best economics book I've ever read.

My wife Marilyn has helped in so many ways I couldn't possibly count them much less describe them.

Roberto Veitia gave me many opportunities to write and speak about economics. Bill Snavely's faith in me gave me confidence. Marshall Fritz and Barry Conner gave me enthusiasm. Karl Hess gave me optimism.

Speaking of confidence, nothing helps a writer so much as other writers, editors and publishers recommending his work or reprinting it. Many thanks to Larry Abraham, Jim Blanchard, Doug Casey, Jim Cook, Richard Fink, John Fund, Mike Ketcher, Al Owen, Robert Prechter, Howard Ruff, Jerry Schomp, Hans Sennholz, William Simon, Mark Skousen, Larry Spears, Diego Veitia, Chris Weber, and Chip Wood.

Contents

*"...All the perplexities,
confusion and distress
in America arise,
not from the defects in their
constitution or confederation,
not from want of honor or virtue,
so much as from downright
ignorance of the nature of
coin, credit and circulation..."*

John Quincy Adams, 1829

Preface

This book is written for people who think economics, business or money is beyond them and best left to experts.

As a technique to keep the explanations as clear and simple as possible, the book is in the form of a series of letters which might have been written by the uncle of a ninth-grade student. The student has asked about inflation and recession, and the uncle, an economist, is answering.

When possible, the letters explain by describing historical events. These cover both ancient and modern history, with special attention to the Roman Empire.

Topics include:
>   money, its origin and history
>   the dollar, its origin and history
>   the business cycle
>   inflation
>   recession
>   depression
>   foreign currencies
>   government, its economic behavior
>   and others

All explanations and interpretations are according to the Austrian and Monetarist schools of economic theory. ("Austrian" because the founders of this school of thought were from Austria, and "Monetarist" because these economists place great importance on the quantity of money circulating in the economy.)

The Austrian school has recently become quite influential. Austrian economist Alan Greenspan has been made Chairman of the Federal Reserve system. Nobel prizes have been awarded to Austrian economists Friedrich A. Hayek, in 1974, and James M. Buchanan in 1986.

The Monetarist school, or as it is sometimes called, the Chicago school, is also gaining acceptance. Its chief spokesman is the 1976 Nobel prize winner, Milton Friedman.

Note to Reader
Throughout the book, when a word that appears in the glossary is introduced in the text, it is displayed in a **bold typeface**.

A Note About Economics

Despite its reputation, economics is neither a "dismal science" nor a difficult field of study. Economics is fascinating and easy to understand, except when someone presents it in a boring or difficult way.

In order to make this book as interesting and understandable as possible, I sought the advice of dozens of students as well as business managers and investors. No concept was included until it was declared to be clear and easy to understand.

As mentioned in the preface, the book is based on Austrian and Monetarist economics. These viewpoints were chosen because good science — good physics, good biology, good chemistry and good economics — depends upon the ability to predict.

In other words, if a physicist correctly predicts the moment at which a projectile will strike its target, or a biologist correctly predicts the effect a change in temperature will have on a population of insects, then we can say that those scientists are using good science. On the other hand, if the predictions are wrong, then the science is flawed.

Economics is subject to the same evaluation. If an economists' predictions are accurate, then his economics must be in tune with the "real world." If his predictions are in error, then his economics must be in error.

This writer believes the predictions of the Austrians and Monetarists have been the most accurate of the economic predictions available today.

Portions of this book have also appeared in other articles and books I have written.

- Richard Maybury

SMART

My dad gave me one dollar bill
'Cause I'm his smartest son,
And I swapped it for two shiny quarters
'Cause two is more than one!

And then I took the quarters
And traded them to Lou
For three dimes — I guess he don't know
That three is more than two!

Just then, along came old blind Bates
And just 'cause he can't see
He gave me four nickels for my three dimes,
And four is more than three!

And I took the nickels to Hiram Coombs
Down at the seed-feed store,
And the fool gave me five pennies for them,
And five is more than four!

And then I went and showed my dad,
And he got red in the cheeks
And closed his eyes and shook his head —
Too proud of me to speak!

Shel Silverstein
Where the Sidewalk Ends

1

Money: Coins and Paper

Dear Chris:

In your last letter you asked me to explain inflation and recession. You said newspapers have been discussing these things and you don't understand what it's all about.

Don't feel alone. Inflation and recession are things most people complain about but few understand. They know their careers, businesses and investments are affected profoundly every day, but they don't know exactly how. Even teachers, newsmen, and politicians are often confused. They know these things are dangerous, but they can't figure out where it all came from or where it's all going.

I'll do my best to explain as clearly as possible. You'll not only learn some important things about your future, but you'll be able to tell others about theirs. You'll also be much better able to become successful in whatever career, business or investments you choose. And, you'll be much better able to stay successful — you'll know the hazards that are out there waiting to ambush you. As they say, forewarned is forearmed.

Before you can understand inflation and recession, you must understand money. So don't read any farther until you get a penny, nickel, dime, quarter, half-dollar, and dollar bill. Lay them in front of you and look at them carefully.

Notice the penny and nickel have no grooves on the edges like the other coins do. Those grooves are called reeding and, believe it or not, they play a part in inflation and recession.

Next look at the edges of the reeded coins. Notice there is copper sandwiched between a nickel-zinc metal. These are called **clad** coins, because the copper and nickel-zinc are clad together. Before 1965 these coins were not clad, they were made entirely of 900 **fine silver**. That's silver which is 90 percent pure. The other ten percent is some **base** (not precious) metal which was added to make the coin hard.

You'll notice none of your dimes, quarters, or halves are dated before 1965. That's because of inflation and recession, and I'll explain it later.

Also, something you probably didn't know is that none of the coins you are looking at are really coins. They are **tokens**. A coin is a disk of precious metal, like gold or silver. If the disk contains no precious metal, it is a token. However, I'll call them coins because that's what you are used to.

Now look at the dollar bill. Notice just above Washington's picture it says, "Federal Reserve Note." Years ago this said "Silver Certificate," and I'll be explaining why it was changed to its present form.

Now look to the left of Washington and notice, "This note is legal tender for all debts public and private." Remember legal tender. It's important, and I'll be explaining why.

All the things you've just observed are directly connected to inflation and recession. In my next letter I'll begin explaining how. First I'll tell you about inflation, then recession.

I'll cover lots of different ideas, then I'll tie them all together in my final letters.

Uncle Eric

2

Tanstaafl, the Romans and Us

Dear Chris,

During the 1970's most of western civilization, and even some eastern countries like Japan, experienced a **double-digit inflation**. Double-digit means that each year prices are rising at the rate of ten (a double-digit number) percent or more.

For instance, during a double-digit inflation, a magazine which cost you $1.00 last year would cost you $1.10 or more this year.

Inflation this serious and this widespread had not happened in the United States since this country became a nation (with the exception of the inflation of the Confederate dollar during the Civil War). However, it was almost this widespread about 20 centuries ago, during the days of the Roman Empire. I'll tell you about the trouble the Romans had. You'll see there's nothing new about inflation or recession; the Romans were plagued by them, too. In fact, these were old problems when the Romans had them. The Greeks had things messed up five centuries before the Romans did.

In Rome it all started with the government. The Roman government behaved pretty much like any other government. It had public works projects, like road and bridge building. It had wars. And it also had welfare programs.

A **welfare program** is the practice of giving things to poor people. Modern governments also have welfare for rich people; that kind of welfare is called a **subsidy**. For instance, if you are a poor person, and the government gives you food, money, medical care or housing, that's welfare. If you are a rich person or a big corporation, and the government gives you land, money, or buildings, that's a subsidy.

Unfortunately the Roman government had a problem. It ran up against a law of economics. A **law of economics** is like a fact of life. It's something you have to live with because you cannot change it.

The law the Romans ran into is a big one. Its slang name is **tanstaafl**, (sounds like tans-t-awful) which means There Ain't No Such Thing As A Free Lunch.

Tanstaafl means that nothing of value is free. Someone must pay for it, if not with money, then with time and hard work. For instance, not even air is free; people work hard and spend lots of money to keep it clean enough to breathe. Tanstaafl was a popular saying during the Great Depression, and it's becoming popular again.

The Roman government wanted tools, land, and gravel for its roads, and it had to pay for these things. It wanted horses and weapons for its soldiers to fight wars, and it had to pay for them. It wanted food and clothing for its welfare programs, and it had to pay for them, too. There ain't no such thing as a free lunch.

The Roman government needed lots of money to buy the things it wanted. The way all governments, including the Roman government, get the money they want is by taxing people. **Taxing** means taking money, by force if necessary, and that's what the Roman government did: tax, tax, tax, take, take, take.

People do not like being taxed -- they do not want the government to take their money. They hate taxes. Everyone does. The Roman people were no exception.

The Roman government soon discovered a very unpleasant fact: when taxes get too high, people get mad enough to revolt and overthrow the government — as the colonists did during the American Revolution.

The Roman government dared not raise taxes any further, but it still needed money to pay for all the things it wanted. That was a tough problem, and most modern governments have the same problem today. How to get money without raising taxes?

However, there was a solution. The Roman government discovered counterfeiting. **Counterfeiting** is the making of phony money.

The usual way to counterfeit nowadays is to print phony money on a printing press. But 20 centuries ago the printing press had not yet been invented. All money was metal coins, and the government had to make phony coins. This is how it was done.

The main coin used in the Roman Empire was the denarius, which was 940 fine silver (94 percent silver). When the tax collectors brought the coins into the Roman government's treasury, the government would have the coins clipped. **Clipping** a coin means shaving the edges off.

Silver Denarius 81-96 AD Rome Domitian

The shavings from the clipped coins were used to mint new coins. The government would then have not only the clipped coins, but the new coins, too. It had a lot more money to buy the things it wanted.

But the Roman people were not stupid. They soon realized that some of their coins were too small and light. Some of the silver was missing. They either refused the clipped coins, or they reduced the value.

For instance, if you wanted a loaf of bread, and the price was one denarius, the baker would either refuse to accept a clipped denarius, or he would demand two clipped coins as a substitute for one whole coin.

In later centuries, people developed an easy method for telling if a coin was clipped. They had notches cut into the edges of the coins. The coins were **reeded**. Any clipped coin was easily recognized because the reeding was gone.

As you can see on your dimes, quarters, and half-dollars, reeding is still a practice today. Base-metal coins, like your pennies and nickels are not reeded because no one ever clips them. But precious-metal coins like dimes, quarters, and halves, which did contain silver until 1965, are reeded. Our clad coins are reeded so they will look like silver coins.

Since reeding made the clipping obvious, a new system of counterfeiting was started. When a denarius was brought into the treasury, it was melted down. Some base-metal like copper was added in. The new coins were minted out of the mixture. A denarius might come into the mint being 94 percent silver, and then go out being only 84 percent silver. Since less silver was used in each coin, more coins could be made, and the politicians had more money to spend.

Every year coins were melted and reminted, with a little more base-metal mixed in each time. This is called **debasing** the money, and it went on for many years.

In 54 A.D. a denarius was 94 percent silver. By 218 A.D. it was down to 43 percent, and only fifty years later it was less than one percent. Look at your half-dollar. In 1964 it was ninety percent silver. Five years later it was down to forty percent. Today it contains no silver.

The Roman people knew their money was losing its silver. So whenever they got a coin with a lot of silver in it, they would save it. They would only spend low-silver coins. The high-silver coins were not used to buy things, while the low-silver coins were used a lot. Only low-silver coins circulated. High-silver coins were hoarded, hidden away.

Gresham's Law was in action. **Gresham's Law** is a law of economics which says: bad money drives good money out of circulation (out of use). In other words, people always save good money, and buy things with bad money. They want to keep the good money, and they want to get rid of the bad money.

For instance, in 1965, Gresham's Law started working in the U.S. When the debased American coins were made, people saved the old silver coins, and spent the new clad coins. (The government's law says people are not allowed to reduce the value of their debased coins. If a coin says 25¢ then it must trade at 25¢ even if it's not made of silver.)

The silver coins all disappeared, and now only clad coins are used. The silver coins are all being saved by people who know that silver is more valuable than copper or nickel. You may know someone who has saved silver coins. Lots of people did and that's what caused the coin shortage of the 1960's.

Remember, the Roman government had to pay for what it bought, but it didn't want to raise taxes to get the money, so the politicians started counterfeiting.

More about the Romans in my next letter.

Uncle Eric

3

Inflation

Dear Chris,

The debasement of the denarius had bad results. Each time the politicians minted more coins, they increased the number of coins in circulation. So what?

Well, have you ever heard of the **law of supply and demand**? The law of supply and demand says that when the supply of something goes up, the value per unit of that thing goes down. For instance, everybody uses pencils, but there are so many pencils that they cost only about ten cents each. If there were only one pencil in the whole world, it would probably be worth a fortune.

The law of supply and demand affects money just as it affects pencils and everything else. If there is very little money, the money is very valuable, and it will buy a great deal. But if there is a lot of money, then it is not so valuable, and it will buy very little.

That's what happened to the Roman money. The politicians counterfeited so much of it that it became almost worthless. In 54 A.D., one denarius might have bought one loaf of bread. But by 268 A.D., so many denarii had been made that it took hundreds to buy a loaf of bread. Every time the number of denarii rose, each individual denarius lost some of its value. That's inflation.

Inflation is an increase in the amount of money. Inflating (increasing) the supply of money causes the value of each unit of the money to go down. When the value of the money goes down, you need more of it to buy what you want. Prices rise.

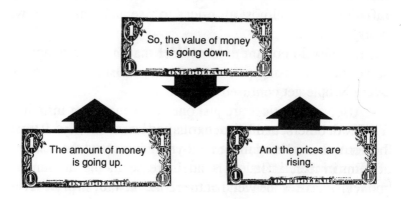

So, the value of money is going down.

The amount of money is going up.

And the prices are rising.

In the Roman Empire it was not the value of food, clothing and other things which was going up. It was the value of the denarius which was going down. Bread didn't cost 300 denarii because the bread was so valuable, it cost 300 denarii because the denarii were almost worthless.

The same thing is happening today. It is happening not only to the dollar, but to almost all money; British, French, Italian, you name it. All over the world, government officials are creating so much money that the money is losing its value. Prices are rising almost everywhere.

In 1968 there were about 200 billion dollars in the United States. Prices were not very high. Today there are already more than 950[1] billion dollars, and prices are up.

---

[1] According to the M1 measure of money supply which counts currency, checking accounts and travelers checks.

Extra money has been created because the people who run the government are using it to pay for what they buy. I'll explain this more in another letter.

It's important to remember that even during times when there is no inflation, some prices rise (and others fall). But inflation causes almost all prices to rise and that's why we worry about it.

It is also important to remember that inflation is not the same thing as rising prices. Inflation **causes** rising prices. Some people get confused about this.

Also, rising prices are just one consequence of inflation. There are others, and I'll be explaining them shortly. Before I go into them, I'm going to tell you more about the dollar.

Remember, inflation is an increase in the amount of money. It causes the value of the money to fall, so prices rise.

Now you know why you can't easily buy a piece of candy for a penny the way your mother could when she was your age. The candy didn't go up, the penny went down.

Uncle Eric

4

Dollars, Money
and Legal Tender

Dear Chris,

What is a dollar? If you think one of those slips of paper in your wallet is a dollar, you've been misled.

I have on my desk a one-ounce ingot of silver. That little silver bar is a dollar. If you're surprised, don't feel alone. You are not the only person who is mistaken.

Most people think that the slip of paper in their wallet is a dollar because the slip says "One Dollar." It sounds logical but think about it for a moment. If I printed up some slips of paper which said "One Basketball," would these slips of paper be basketballs? Of course not.

ONE BASKETBALL

Let's see where the dollar came from.

For about 40 centuries gold has been used as money. Silver has also served the purpose for about 25 centuries. There are good reasons why people use these two metals as money.

But first, what is money?

Money is the most easily traded item. Of course you can trade almost anything — pencils, TV sets, baseballs, comic books, marbles — anything. But all things are not easily traded. They are either not easily moved, like a house, or their value is not easy to figure, like a diamond. Or they are not desired by many people, like limburger cheese. Or they rust or rot away too easily, like iron.

In fact, very few things are small, easy to move, widely desired, and corrosion-proof. And very few things are scarce and hard to copy. But good money must have these characteristics.

Throughout the centuries only two things have been found which make good money: gold and silver. People have tried, and are still trying, almost everything else. But they always come back to gold and silver. Nothing works better. Also, the fact that both metals have long been used as jewelry means people attach a special significance to them — they're beautiful and precious.

Some strange things have been used for money. People have tried not only paper but stones, cattle, beads, salt, fish, and even sea shells. But gold and silver are still the favorites.

However, there is a problem with gold and silver. When you use a piece of gold or silver as money, how do you know how much you have? How do you know the weight and the purity?

Fortunately the invention of the coin solved the problem.

Coins were invented because they help a person tell how much gold or silver he has.

A real **coin** is a disk of gold or silver. It has three things stamped on it: the weight of the coin, the fineness of the metal, and the name of the mint which made the coin. The name of the mint is the **hallmark.** The hallmark tells you how good the coin is, just as the names Cadillac, Rolls Royce, and Chevrolet tell you how good a car is.

If the hallmark of a coin was Jones and you knew the Jones mint made good coins, then you would trust the weight and fineness of the coin. You would willingly take a Jones coin in trade for your goods or services.

For instance, if a baker wanted one ounce of silver for a loaf of bread, and if the Jones mint made a half-ounce coin which the baker trusted, then the price of the bread would be two Joneses.

Back during the middle ages there was a mint in a place called Joachimthal, in Bohemia. That's in Czechoslovakia. The Joachimthal mint made a one-ounce silver coin, and the coin, called a Joachimthaler, was widely accepted as a very good coin. The name Joachimthaler was eventually shortened to thaler.

The thaler was such a good coin that everyone wanted it. Thaler came to mean the same thing as one ounce of silver. Instead of saying one ounce of silver, people would say one thaler.

For instance, in exchange for a haircut, a barber might charge one ounce of silver, or he might charge one thaler. It was the same thing.

As you've already guessed, thaler was changed to daler, which eventually came to be dollar. In other words, dollar means one ounce of silver.

Other names of other monies also meant weights of gold or silver. The best example is the British Pound Sterling, which meant one pound of sterling (925 fine) silver. A French Franc meant one one-hundredths of an ounce of gold. The gold shekel of Babylon was a half-ounce of gold. A silver shekel was a half-ounce of silver.

Unfortunately, all money has one big problem: safety and storage. When you're not using it, where do you put it to keep it from being lost or stolen?

Another invention, the money warehouse, solved the problem. When people weren't using their gold or silver, they would store it in a money warehouse. When a person put his money into the warehouse, the warehouse owner would give him a receipt for it. The receipt might say something like, "This certifies that there is on deposit in the Smith Warehouse one-hundred thalers, payable to the bearer on demand." It was a kind of IOU.

The money warehouses became banks and a **banknote** was an IOU from the bank. Anyone who had a banknote could take it to the bank and get his gold or silver. An IOU for one ounce of silver was a one dollar banknote. An IOU for one one-hundredth ounce of gold was a one franc banknote.

Until the 1960's the slips of paper in your wallet were still one dollar banknotes. They were not Federal Reserve Notes. They were called Silver Certificates. Any time you felt like it you could take them to the U.S. Treasury and get silver for them. The older silver certificates had no legal tender statement. Instead they said: "This certifies that there is on Deposit in the Treasury of the United States of America One Dollar in Silver Payable to the Bearer on Demand."

Until the 1960's, the U.S. dollar was a very good money. People all over the world wanted it because it could be exchanged for a precious metal. But that has changed. The U.S. dollar is not so popular now. The reason?

The Silver Certificates are gone. The government printed too many of them. In order to pay for the things it was buying, the government printed so many paper dollars that it didn't have enough silver or gold to back them. Now it prints only Federal Reserve Notes, because they are not IOUs for anything. They are just paper, and they are being printed in large quantities.

So why aren't they worthless? What gives them value?

The legal tender statement. To understand, we must go back to the year 1270 A.D.

Back in 1270 A.D. a government which ruled much of Asia was led by Kublai Khan. Kublai Khan wanted to buy many things for his government but he was afraid to raise taxes to get enough money.

He wanted silver and gold very badly, so he invented paper money, "paper gold," as a substitute. If he needed twenty ounces of gold to buy something, he would write "Twenty Ounces of Gold" on a slip of paper, and sign his name to it.

At first people refused to accept the paper money. So Kublai Khan passed a legal tender law. Under the **legal tender law**, anyone who refused to take the paper money was punished. Kublai Khan could be a pretty mean guy, and everyone was scared of him, so they accepted his paper money in trade for their goods. Legal tender money is sometimes called **fiat money**.

About 200 years ago, the French government was doing the same thing Kublai Khan had done. It was printing phony money, and backing up that money with a legal tender law. If a person refused to accept the paper money in trade for his goods or services, his head was chopped off by the guillotine.

Fortunately, in the U.S. the punishment is not that bad. If someone owes you money, and you refuse to take Federal Reserve Notes in payment of the debt, then the debt is cancelled. The person does not have to pay you.

However, it was not always that way. Two hundred years ago anyone who violated the legal tender law was charged with treason and thrown in jail. That was during the Revolutionary War, when the government was inflating by printing the Continental Dollars. The paper Continentals became worthless (although, of course, the silver and gold money kept its value), and the people did not forget it for a long time. That's part of the reason behind the first sentence of Article One, Section Ten of the U.S. Constitution.

ARTICLE 1, SECTION 10
U.S. Constitution
(First Paragraph Only)

No State shall enter into any Treaty, Alliance, or Confederation; grant Letters of Marque and Reprisal; coin Money; emit Bills of Credit; <u>make any Thing but gold and silver Coin a Tender in Payment of Debts</u>; pass any Bill of Attainder, ex post facto Law, or Law impairing the Obligation of Contracts, or grant any Title of Nobility. [emphasis added]

That sentence is one of the many examples of people trying to stop history from being repeated.

If you're interested in the Revolutionary War, you might like to know what happened to George Washington at Valley Forge. Washington was angry at the local farmers and merchants because they were raising prices so high that Washington could not buy enough food and clothing for his men. According to his letters, he thought the farmers and merchants were taking unfair advantage of his situation.

Washington, at that time, apparently did not know that the government was paying for the war by printing enormous amounts of Continentals. Prices were rising because the money was becoming worth less. Anyone who tried to use Continental Dollars to buy something found that no one would accept his money unless he was willing to pay a lot.

On the other hand, anyone who had gold or silver, or some other noninflated money, was not bothered by rising prices. So the winter at Valley Forge would not have been so bad for Washington and his men if they had had better money.

During the two hundred years since Valley Forge, the government has issued many kinds of dollars. The Continental Dollar was not the only dollar destroyed by inflation. The Civil War Greenback Dollar of the 1860s lost much of its value and the Confederate Dollar was entirely destroyed by inflation. The Gold Certificate Dollar and the Silver Certificate Dollar were not destroyed by inflation, but they have been replaced by the Federal Reserve Dollar which has already been severely damaged.

Until the 1930's the government allowed gold coins to circulate, and until the 1960's silver coins also circulated. Neither was seriously damaged by inflation because, as you know, gold and silver cannot be created on a printing press.

Chris, now is a good time to let you know that economic problems are only symptoms, the cause is law. Inflation, recessions, business failures, unemployment and poverty are caused fundamentally by corruption of America's legal system.

The legal system we have today is not the one America's founders intended.

Political law is all sword and no principles.

I can't stress strongly enough how important it is for you to understand how today's legal system effects the economy. I promise we'll talk about this in future letters[2], but first we must finish our discussion about economics.

In my next letter I'll tell you about politics and printing presses. Remember money is valuable because people are willing to take it in trade for their goods and services. If people will not trade for it, then it's not money.

Uncle Eric

---

[2] See WHATEVER HAPPENED TO JUSTICE? by Richard J. Maybury, published by Bluestocking Press, 1993. A series of letters from "Uncle Eric" to Chris about how the current legal system effects the economy.

5

Revolutions, Elections
and Printing Presses

Dear Chris,

In an earlier letter I told you I'd explain more about why government inflates.

It's a fact of life that all governments inflate. They always have. There might be a few exceptions to this, but they are too small and too short-lived to be of any significance.

Both democracies and dictatorships inflate, some more than others.

Dictators inflate because they fear revolutions. They must not raise taxes too much or they risk being overthrown or assassinated. So instead of raising taxes, they print money. They inflate.

In a democracy like the U.S., revolutions are not a problem, but elections are.

In a democracy, people who run for office get elected by promising what the people want. That's fine. However, people's wants are unlimited, so politicians are constantly promising more, and more, and more.

For instance, suppose you and I are both running for the Senate. I am trying to get enough votes to beat you, and you are trying to beat me.

I might promise the voters new schools and new highways. You reply by promising new schools, new highways, and new hospitals.

When it looks as if you might win, I offer even more. I promise not only schools, highways, and hospitals, but parks, and playgrounds, too. Since I promise more, the voters elect me.

Keep in mind that the voters always elect the person who comes closest to offering what they want. The only way a person can get elected is to promise what the people want.

Now I am in office and I must give the people what I promised. If I don't I'll be a liar. The people will vote against me in the next election.

Of course I can't raise taxes enough to pay for all the things I promised. I'd make a lot of enemies and they'd vote me out of office. If I raised taxes a lot, they might even have me impeached.

So I start printing money. I start inflating.

However, modern politicians don't just run the printing presses. They use a more complex system. They use the banks and Federal Reserve. You don't need to know how it works, all you need to know is that it does the same thing. It increases the amount of money, and that makes the money worth less. Prices rise.

(If you'd like to know more about how the banks and Federal Reserve are used to inflate, the clearest explanation I've ever read was in the first 100 pages of Harry Browne's 1971 best-seller HOW YOU CAN PROFIT FROM THE COMING DEVALUATION. Call a bookstore or your local library.)

No matter where you go, the story is the same. In Russia, in China, England, Japan, even in Switzerland, there is inflation. All governments inflate. In my next letter I'll tell you about the wage/price spiral.

Remember inflation, like taxes, is just one of the many prices we pay for a large, powerful government. It's always been that way and probably always will be.

Uncle Eric

Modern politicians don't just run the printing presses to inflate. Today they use the banks and federal reserve.

6

Wages, Prices, Spirals and Controls

Dear Chris,

In one of your letters you asked what people mean when they talk about the wage/price spiral. You also asked about wage/price controls.

The wage/price spiral is a mistaken idea of what causes inflation. Some people think prices rise because of the following events:

By joining unions and going on strike, workers get higher wages. Then businesses must raise the prices of their goods so they can get the money to pay the higher wages.

The workers see the higher prices. They demand higher wages so they can pay the higher prices. Then the business managers must raise prices further to pay the higher wages.

For instance, the managers of Ford and Chrysler raise the prices of their cars. The workers cannot buy the higher priced cars, so they demand higher wages. The managers must then raise the prices of the cars to pay the higher wages. Around and around they go, first a strike, then a price increase, then another strike, then another price increase, and so forth. Wages and prices spiral upward.

The wage/price spiral sounds logical, but you must ask a question. Where did the money come from?

Chrysler can *ask* any price it wants for its cars, from ten dollars to ten million dollars. But it will only get the money if the money exists. Where did the money come from?

An auto worker can *demand* any salary, from ten dollars per hour to ten million dollars per hour. But he will only get the money if the money exists. Where did the money come from?

The answer, of course, is that someone printed it.

If the supply of money had not changed, then the only way for one person to have more money would be for someone else to have less. When one worker's wages went up, another worker's wages would have to go down. When one business's prices went up, another business's prices would have to go down. The value of your money would not change.

The only way for all wages and prices to go up is for someone to print money. If the money is not being printed, then each rise in a wage or price would have to be matched by a fall in some other wage or price.

For instance, if the amount of money does not change, and the price of oil rises, then the prices of comic books, records, clothes, and other items must fall. That's because people are using more money to buy oil, so they have less money left over to buy other things (see *The Oil Myth,* page 89).

Also, remember if inflation is taking place then the inflated money is becoming worth less. Any business or worker who doesn't demand more is crazy.

Another approach helps us understand why the wage/price spiral is a result, not a cause, of inflation. Remember your grandfather.

When your grandfather was a young man he was willing

to work for 25¢ per hour. His new car cost only $400. But today a new car can cost $10,000 or more and workers like your grandfather can earn upwards of $10 per hour.

So why did the workers and auto companies wait until today to raise wages and prices that high? Why not spiral the wages and prices up quickly, and get all that money right away? Because employers and car buyers did not have the money to pay that much. They did not have the money because the money had not yet been created. The supply of money in the U.S. during your grandfather's day was much less than now.

If someone demands money faster than it is created, he simply won't get it. No one will have it to give to him. That's why workers aren't demanding ten million dollars per hour and Chrysler isn't demanding ten million dollars per car. That much money doesn't exist. Yet.

But don't get the wrong impression. Some businesses try to raise prices faster than the government inflates. When that happens, many customers don't have the money to buy the businesses' products, so the businesses either go broke or bring their prices back down again. Remember, too, that price increases are not always related to inflation. Not all prices reflect inflation to the same extent or at the same time.

And unions often try to push wages up faster than the government inflates. But then the employers don't have the money to hire all the workers, or some workers have no jobs. Either they are replaced by machines, or their jobs are simply abolished and the product they once made is no longer sold. If you ever go to England, Italy or New York City, you'll see that happening a lot.

Of course it is possible for workers to get money a little faster than the government inflates, but they must earn it.

They must produce more goods or services to sell, either by using better tools or by working harder. TANSTAAFL.

Unfortunately most businesses, especially the big corporations, pay so many taxes that they don't have enough money left over to buy better tools for all the workers. So the only way for the workers to earn money faster than the government inflates is to work harder.

Sometimes the workers do not understand all this, and so they strike for much higher wages. Then their employer goes broke, and lots of workers lose their jobs. Railroads, like the Penn Central, have had that problem a lot.

But a more common problem is the situation in the California grape fields. The workers who pick grapes allowed their union to push wages up rapidly. I guess they didn't understand that if the price of their labor goes up, the demand for their labor will go down.

One grape farmer used to hire 40 workers to pick his grapes. But now the workers' wages are high enough that it is cheaper for the farmer to buy a machine to pick the grapes. So now the farmer only hires two workers. Of course these two workers are enjoying their high wages, and they are grateful to their union, but the other 38 have no jobs. The law of supply and demand cannot be violated.

Now let's talk about wage/price controls. Sometimes during an inflation, government will forbid people to raise wages or prices. In all the history of the world, it has never worked.

If the amount of money goes up enough, the value per unit goes down. Period. That's a fact and no one can change it.

If the people are not allowed to increase their prices or wages during an inflation, they quit working. When the value of the money goes down, and they can't get more of it to make up for the loss, they go on strike. Why should people continue making food, clothing, or anything else when the value of the money they get for their work is going down, down, down?

During wage/price controls, people stop making the food, clothing, houses, lamps, pencils, and other things they are working on. Shortages develop.

For instance, the Roman government tried wage/price controls. Food price increases were taboo. After a while, the money the farmers were getting for their crops lost much of its value because the inflation had not stopped. The farmers quit farming. There was a shortage of food. People starved to death.

When the Roman government halted the wage/price controls, the farmers went back to work and the famine was over.

Even today, people sometimes ask their government to start controlling wages and prices. The results are always the same. Shortages happen, and the tighter the controls are, the worse the shortages are.

Sometimes, if the wage/price controls last long enough, an illegal or "black" market develops. A **black market** is the buying, selling, or making of something against the wishes of the government or above the prices the government allows.

For instance, in California, the government does not allow gambling, so the people who gamble are taking part in the black market. In Nevada gambling is legal, so there is no black market for gambling in that state. Many years ago, during prohibition, liquor was illegal, it became a black market product. Today it is legal, and it is no longer part of the black market. In many parts of the world, things like marijuana, guns and pornography are black market products, because they are illegal.

During wage/price controls people still must earn a living. So they often produce and trade things at prices which are illegally high: they start a black market.

For example, during 1976 in Iran it was illegal to sell a certain car for more than $4200. But the auto dealers still had to earn a living, so they sold the cars"under the counter" for $5700. They were careful not to get caught.

Also during World War II the U.S. Government paid for much of the guns and other war goods by printing money. As the new money moved from person to person, prices started rising — because the money was losing its value — and the government tried to stop the rise by using price controls.

However, the politicians did not stop printing money, so the money kept losing its value. A black market developed. All kinds of things — tires, silk stockings, gasoline, oil and many others — were bought and sold in the black market.

No one knows how big the black market is today in the U.S. I've seen estimates that run from a low of 5% up to 20% of all goods and servcies bought and sold.

In countries like Britain, Italy and France, the black market is believed to be even larger. And, as taxes and controls increase, the black markets will grow, because more goods and services will be traded secretly.

Despite all the things I've already described to you, there are still some people who believe the wage/price spiral is a cause, not a result, of inflation. They believe wage/price controls are a good idea. If these people would study enough history, I am willing to bet they would discover three things which would change their minds:

(1) Large increases in the supply of money are always followed by increases in wages and prices. (Small increases in the supply of money do not always cause a change in wages or prices because other things can be more influential.) Even

when there are no unions and no big industries, this is still true.

(2) Large decreases in the supply of money are always followed by a fall in wages and prices. Even when there are powerful unions and giant industries, this is still true. (Except when the unions will not allow wages to fall; then some of the workers lose their jobs because the employers cannot afford to pay them. That almost happened to me once).

(3) With only a very few exceptions, there has never been a case where wages and prices rose rapidly without someone creating a lot of money.

One exception happened during the 1500s and 1600s, when the Spanish conquistadors were stealing the Aztecs' and Incas' gold and silver. The conquistadors stole so much gold and silver, and sent so much back to Europe, that the money supply in Europe rose quite a bit. So wages and prices rose in Europe. When the Aztecs and Incas ran out of gold and silver, European wages and prices leveled off. The gold discoveries in California and Australia (1848+) and in Alaska (1896-1902) were also inflations which affected prices.

I guess even today the same thing could happen if enough money was moved from one part of the world to another. But I don't know of any such cases except a few small incidents in Switzerland. Sometimes there will be a war or some other trouble somewhere and people will move a lot of their money into Switzerland. The Swiss are occasionally bothered by that, but not like the Europeans were 400 years ago.

Remember the wage/price spiral is a result, not a cause of inflation. The general, over-all level of wages and prices cannot rise unless someone creates more money. Wage/price controls have never worked because they could not stop the money supply from increasing.

Next I'll tell you about runaway inflation.

Uncle Eric

7

Wallpaper, Wheelbarrows and Recessions

Dear Chris,

By now you're probably saying, "But the world's governments cannot keep creating money forever. They must stop sometime. Prices can't rise forever!"

Let's look again at history. Inflation isn't an unusual event. In fact, it's quite common. I'd say it happens about as often as major wars, earthquakes, and other troubles.

When an inflation gets bad enough for prices to be rising rapidly, every few hours, it's called a **runaway inflation**. For instance, a few runaway inflations of the past are:

Nation	Year
American Colonies	1775-1781
France	1796
U.S.A.	1865
Germany	1923
Russia	1924
Hungary	1946
China	1949
Indonesia	1965
Brazil	1971
Mexico	1980s
Poland	1990s
Russia	1990s

Keep in mind that these are not just double-digit inflations, they are runaway inflations. Much worse.

For instance, in Germany a pound of butter cost 1.4 marks
in 1914. By 1918 the price was up to 3.0 marks. Four years
later it was 2400 marks, and the next year it was
6,000,000,000,000 (six trillion!) marks. In 1914 one egg cost
less than one mark. Nine years later an egg was
80,000,000,000 (eighty billion marks).

In the Hungarian inflation of 1946, the money lost all its
value. You could wallpaper a room more cheaply with money
than with wallpaper. It took so much money to buy things that
people had to carry their cash in wheelbarrows.

Sometimes governments will even try to use runaway
inflation as a weapon of war. During World War II the
German government counterfeited millions of British pounds,
and rumor has it that the British and American governments
were printing German marks, and the Russians were printing
U.S. money.

But runaway inflations usually happen because, once
started, an inflation is hard to stop. To see why, let's look at
an easy example. I'll make up a story. To keep things simple,

I'll talk only about your home town, and I'll assume the inflating is done by a counterfeiter rather than a government.

Pretend you are the owner of a record shop in your home town, and I am your friendly local counterfeiter. I begin printing money to pay my bills, just as government does, and I am generous enough to share it with my friends, just like the government.

My friends change their spending habits. So long as producers and/or outsiders continue to supply more products, my friends are no longer satisfied buying hamburgers and Volkswagens. Instead they buy steaks and Cadillacs. They also use their extra money to buy lots of records.

Shortly after I begin printing money, you notice the demand for records has gone way up. Being a wise merchant, you take advantage of the opportunity. You expand your business. You buy plenty of records. You hire more clerks. You buy a larger building.

Everyone is happy — until prices start rising. Being a concerned citizen, I am upset over the fact that my inflation is destroying the value of my friends' money. I stop printing money. By this time, too, the suppliers are balking at accepting any more paper money.

Suddenly the demand for records goes back down. Fewer people are buying records. Your extra clerks have no work to do, so you must fire them. You have too many records, so you must sell them at a loss. You must sell your large store and move back to the small one, and the move costs you much time and money.

Unemployment rises while the clerks retrain and look for other jobs. You are losing money. A depression has hit your home town.

In other words, my inflation caused you to make mistakes.

You hired too many people. You unwisely spent your money on a new store and extra records.

Correcting your mistakes meant firing your employees. You were losing money. A depression happened.

A **depression** is the correction period following an inflation. During a depression businesses go broke and people lose their jobs. Many become poorer. It's all caused by the inflation.

Sometimes governments stop inflating, but then they get worried about the depression. They see people out of work, so they start inflating again. That stops the depression for a while.

When a government stops a depression before it gets going, that's a recession. A **recession** is the beginning of a depression that never went all the way.

That's why we have inflation, then recession, then inflation, then recession, and so on. Politicians inflate till they get scared of rising prices. Then they stop inflating until they get scared of the unemployment. Then they start inflating again. That up, down, up, down, up down stuff is called the business cycle.

Each round of inflation causes businessmen to make more mistakes. More corrections are needed. So each recession needs to be worse than the last.

Therefore, each recession needs a little more inflation to stop it, so each inflation must be a little worse than the last.

The severity of a recession depends on how much inflation is slowed. For instance, the 1975 recession was very bad because the inflation had been slowed a lot. Very little money was being created. But the 1970 recession was very mild because inflation slowed very little. The 1982 recession was terrible.

How do you tell the difference between a depression and a recession? An old joke says that if your neighbor loses his job, that's a recession; if you lose your lob, it's a depression.

Really though, it's easy to tell the difference. If the inflation is slowed down or stopped for a few months, it's a recession. If the inflation stops for years, it's a depression. Inflation must be stopped permanently if the economy is to recover on a sound or long term basis.

In fact, depressions usually involve deflations. A **deflation** is when the amount of money goes down, which causes the value of the money to go up. Prices fall.

For now, remember that recessions or depressions are due to the bad policy of inflation. They reveal the mistakes and malinvestments businesses made under the influence of the inflation. Thus recessions or depressions are periods of correction in which business people try to better adjust production and prices to what consumers want.

Even though it appears government is rescuing the economy when it resorts to inflation once more, and brings a recession or depression to an end, it is actually only postponing the end to inflation. It is storing up still more distortion and malinvestment for the future, and making a return to sound money still more difficult.

Many years ago no one understood the business cycle. No one knew what caused it, and some people made all kinds of silly suggestions. For instance, some people thought the business cycle was caused by sunspots.

But today we know the business cycle is caused by the amount of money being shifted up and down.

It's important to remember that the politicians would like to stop inflating. They hate rising prices just as we do. But they have been inflating for many decades and if they stop, a depression will happen. Once in a while they do slow the inflation, or stop it temporarily. That causes a recession, like in 1970, 1975 and 1982. But they are afraid to stop inflation altogether. If I was one of them, I would be too.

The economy is now so disorganized that the number of dollars officials print to forestall depression is probably greater than the number they print to finance their spending.

If you'd like to read about a real case of people making bad decisions -- decisions which had to be corrected -- because of too much money being freely available, an example appeared in a *Wall Street Journal* story March 2, 1978. Ask a librarian for it.

According to this story many people in Atlanta, Georgia, had made bad real estate investments during the early 1970s, when the government was creating a lot of money. Even a few bankers were caught up in the get-rich-quick fever.

Then in 1974, when the government stopped inflating, all these bad investments came to light. Many people were very sorry they hadn't been more careful. Some large companies went broke.

As the people in Atlanta discovered, inflation is like being hooked on heroin. Once you've gotten into it, you can only stop by going through the withdrawals, the depression.

How bad do the withdrawals need to be? I'll tell you later.

Until then, remember that inflation causes recessions and depressions. The only way to never have recessions and depressions is to never inflate.

Also, remember that inflation is like taxes. It's just one of the prices we pay for a big government.

Uncle Eric

8

Fast Money

Dear Chris,

One aspect of inflation which is poorly understood by almost everyone, including some economists, is velocity. In recent years officials have become very concerned about it. Economists in the Federal Reserve discuss it constantly now. Some are also discussing a related topic called money demand.

First I'll say a few words about velocity, then money demand.

Like everything else about economics, velocity is easy to understand if you ignore all the complex theory. Simply think about people. Just keep thinking about the way individual human beings behave.

Many years ago when I was still a student, I asked an economist to tell me about velocity. He said, "Velocity is the component of the Equation of Exchange which is computed by dividing M_1 by PQ." I'll try to be a bit clearer than that here.

The economist meant to say that **velocity** is the speed at which money changes hands. For instance, if a dollar bill is traded once in a year, its velocity is one. If that dollar changes hands five times in a year, then its velocity is five.

Imagine ten people sitting in a circle. Each has two things in his hands, a dollar bill and a baseball card. Now imagine each person selling his card to the person on his right for one dollar. Every card has been sold, and every dollar has changed hands once. The velocity of the money is one.

Now imagine the same circle of ten people. Each has a baseball card but only one person has a dollar. Now imagine the person with the dollar buying his neighbor's card. The neighbor then uses the dollar to buy his neighbor's card. That neighbor uses the dollar to buy his neighbor's card, and so forth. The dollar goes all the way around the circle, each person using it to buy a card.

That single dollar has done the same work as the ten dollars in the first example. All the cards were sold for one dollar. But, the money changed hands not once but ten times. Velocity was ten.

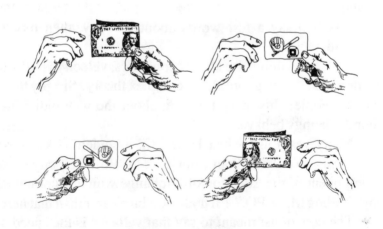

In other words, a small amount of money can do the same work as a large amount. It can be used in the same number of transactions and have the same effect on prices if it changes hands quickly enough.

Why would people trade their money away faster? What would make you trade your money away faster?

A decline in money demand. When I said in an earlier letter that money responds to the law of supply and demand, I meant exactly that. There is a demand for money as well as a supply of it. After all, you want money, right? Most people do.

When demand for the dollar falls, this means people are more willing to spend dollars than to hold them. They buy more goods and services and keep fewer dollars. This has the same effect on prices as an increase in the money supply. People are spending faster, so each dollar is used in more transactions and has more effect on prices.

If demand for the dollar rises, people are more willing to hold dollars and less willing to spend them. Their buying decreases and this has the same effect as an decrease in the money supply. The dollars exist but they aren't being used as much and they aren't affecting prices as much.

A very important point here is that money demand is the cause and velocity is the effect. If money demand falls, the money changes hands faster — the "velocity of circulation" rises; if money demand rises, velocity falls.

Some people speak as if velocity were a force in itself but it's not, it's a *symptom*. When we want to know if the demand for the dollar is rising or falling, we can look at how fast the dollar is changing hands.

Inflation usually goes in three stages. Each stage is caused by a change in money demand. Here are some examples.

FIRST EXAMPLE: Suppose you earn twenty dollars and you want to buy a radio. Last year the radio cost $10.00, but the government has been printing money so the radio has risen to $12.00. You decide to hang onto your money, hoping the radio will come back down to $10.00.

In this first example, you did not spend your money. You held onto your dollars, so they did not circulate. Your demand for dollars was high and the velocity of your dollars was low.

In the first stages of inflation, people save their money, waiting for prices to fall. Because they hold onto their money it doesn't enter the market to bid up prices. Little of the newly printed money is being spent and prices cannot rise very fast.

SECOND EXAMPLE: Suppose you still have your twenty dollars, and officials are still printing money. The price of the radio is up to $15.00, and you decide to buy now before the price goes higher. Your brother, who intended to buy a radio next year, also decides to buy now before the price goes higher.

Notice, your brother has speeded up his buying. He is getting rid of his money faster than he intended to. The money is circulating faster. Demand for dollars has fallen and velocity has increased.

In the second stage of inflation, the money changes hands faster. A little bit of money is beginning to do the work of a lot of money. Prices start rising faster than the money is being printed.

THIRD EXAMPLE: Suppose you earn another twenty dollars. The price of the radio has risen to $20.00. You do not want another radio but your money is losing its value. You know radios are not losing their value. You trade your money for another radio, because you trust the value of radios more than you trust the value of dollars. Your friends and neighbors are doing the same thing. They are buying anything they can find, just so they can get rid of their money before it becomes worthless.

In the third stage of inflation, the money changes hands very fast. People don't want it and they're trying to get rid of it. Money demand is falling like a stone and velocity is skyrocketing.

In the third stage, no one can stop the money from losing its value. Even if the printing presses are stopped, the money becomes worthless because no one wants it.

The third stage is the final, runaway stage of inflation. It is ended when people completely reject the money and begin using something new for money. They usually switch over to a good foreign currency, or to gold or silver. During American runaway inflations, they generally switch over to gold or silver.

If you ever spend some time in a Latin American country, you might get a chance to see inflation go through all three stages. It's very common in places like Brazil, Argentina and Peru. For instance, it happened in Chile during the mid-1970's.

In some parts of the world, the inflation is usually stopped during the second stage. A depression or recession follows immediately. But in the Latin American countries, the inflations often go all the way before the corrections are allowed to begin.

Now that you know about velocity, you may be a little worried about it. You may be wondering what keeps velocity from suddenly going wild and destroying the money. What keeps velocity under control?

The answer is that the people, you and I and everyone else, keep velocity under control. In fact, there is probably no other part of the economy that is as democratically controlled as velocity.

Every person, regardless of race, creed or color, makes

daily decisions about spending his money. Therefore, although he may not realize it, every person makes daily decisions about velocity. If a person spends his money more quickly than usual, velocity increases; if he spends his money more slowly than usual, velocity falls.

Actually though, people do not change their spending habits very much, unless they have a good reason, so velocity seldom varies. However, there are two things which can cause people to change their spending habits enough to change velocity. Either (#1) someone monkeys with the supply of money, or (#2) the government which prints the money and enforces the legal tender laws begins to go out of business.

A good example of #1 happened in the U.S. between 1915 and 1929. During World War I and the 1920's, the government caused a big increase in the supply of money. Those newly created dollars were the main thing that caused the "Roaring Twenties" to roar. The inflation caused stock prices to skyrocket, so millions of people felt rich, temporarily. Few people realized that the inflation which had made them feel so prosperous was setting the stage for the Great Depression.

The inflation caused people to spend their money faster, so during the 1920's, velocity rose. Then during the early 1930's, the Depression era, the government stopped expanding the money supply, and prices fell. People were fearful about losing their jobs, so they avoided spending money, and velocity fell, too.

A good example of #2 happened in Viet Nam during the 1970's. When the North Vietnamese army invaded South Viet Nam, everyone knew that the South Vietnamese government would soon be out of business. The South Vietnamese people realized that no one would be enforcing the legal tender laws.

The Vietnamese money was called the piaster. Demand for it plunged. The Vietnamese began spending their piasters as quickly as possible and the velocity of the money rose violently.

Prices went wild and people tried to trade their piasters for anything. They preferred gold, and some of them fled to the U.S. carrying lots of the yellow metal, but they would take almost anything they could get. It was not unusual for the American airmen who were flying into Viet Nam to be offered large bundles of piasters in exchange for a few U.S. dollars.

A final point. The fact that inflations go through three stages does not mean they go through these stages in an inevitable, mechanical way. They can go from stage one to stage two then back to one again if the government is willing to trigger a recession.

For instance, in the late 1970s the U.S. was in stage two and moving toward stage three. The goverment tightened the money supply, thereby giving us the back-to-back 1980 and 1982 recessions. The '82 recession was the worst since the Great Depression of the 1930s. Money demand stabilized and velocity stopped climbing. In fact, statistics show velocity began falling. Apparently we went back into stage one.

The 1980s were the first time since World War II that velocity had fallen and government economists became quite concerned about it. Many shifted their attention away from money supply to money demand.

Remember, inflation goes through three stages and these stages are caused by changes in money demand. Velocity is a way to know how money demand is changing.

Uncle Eric

9

Getting Rich Quick

Dear Chris,

One of the strangest and most dangerous things about inflation is that it is usually accompanied by fast-action, get-rich-quick fads. The reason isn't hard to understand if we look at an example.

Suppose you live in an area where some powerful politician has gotten elected by promising to build a big new military weapons plant. (The politician won the election because his opponent only promised to build a small weapons plant.)

The new plant is being built, and the government has decided to pay for it by printing money. You leave your $10,000 per year job and take one of the $20,000 jobs at the new plant. So you are receiving thousands of dollars of the newly created money — that's your reward for voting for the politician.

Now that your income has risen, you decide to invest $5000 somewhere. You look around for a good investment and you discover there is a shortage of apartments in nearby Destitutionville. Rents and land prices are rising in that area (remember the law of supply and demand) so you decide to get in on a good thing. You become an apartment owner.

You have many neighbors who are also benefiting from the new weapons plant, and they start buying property in Destitutionville, too. Soon real estate prices in Destitutionville are skyrocketing. Things turned out even better than you expected. Your $5000 has become $50,000.

The real estate buyers who are now arriving in Destitutionville are finding there is no property left to buy. No one will sell because everyone expects prices to keep rising.

The new buyers start building their own apartments. Soon the apartment shortage turns into a surplus. A few pessimists point out that there is no longer any good reason for prices to keep rising, but no one ever listens to a party pooper. Everyone is rich and getting richer, so there is nothing to worry about. All these people can't be mistaken, can they?

They can. All good things must come to an end. The government has decided to quit creating money for awhile because its inflation has led to double-digit price rises. No more new money is being created, so no new money is available for the Destitutionville real estate market. Prices stop rising.

Of course you don't mind the temporary cooling off period. You have a big fat profit, and you are content to wait for the government to start printing money again.

However, the last group of people who bought property have no profits. They bought when prices were already high, and they haven't earned one thin dime. They decide that Destitutionville isn't such a good place to invest after all, so they start selling their property.

Now the panic to get into Destitutionville turns into a panic to get out. You notice prices are starting to fall but you are not worried because you can afford to take a slight loss. But prices keep falling and you eventually join the panic.

Unfortunately, by that time you cannot sell your property; no one is dumb enough to buy when prices are falling. Also, the number of new apartments is so large that half of them are unrented, and rents are falling (supply and demand again).

No matter how low you set your selling price, no one will buy, so you finally realize that your property is worthless. You've not only lost your $45,000 profit, but you've also lost your original $5,000.

Now you are stuck with your worthless property and you must continue paying taxes on it, hoping that someday the government will re-inflate enough for you to get your $5,000 back.

After a few years you realize that the Destitutionville real estate market will probably never recover. You sell your apartments for $200 to a local farmer who tears them down and uses the land to plant corn.

You have learned, the hard way, that get-rich-quick is usually followed by get-poor-quick. But don't feel alone. Every time politicians inflate, millions of people get suckered into fast-buck schemes.

Let's look at this a little closer. Before the inflation starts, some prices are already rising (while some are falling). Every healthy economy has some rising prices because some goods or services are always in shorter supply than others. A rising price is a signal to business people that more of a particular product is needed, and profits are available to anyone who satisfies that need.

When the inflation hits, lots of people are looking for good places to invest their extra dollars; they naturally flock to the investments which are already rising in price. That causes these prices to rise further. More people invest, and the prices rise even more. Prices continue to skyrocket until the supply of new money dries up.

In other words if, for instance, apples are in short supply when an inflation starts, you can expect the price of apples to go far, far above anything reasonable. Those apples will draw money like a magnet draws iron filings.

If inflation is running at five or ten percent, the price of apples might rise at the rate of fifty or a hundred percent, maybe more. That's because the apples are noticeable, their rising price makes them stand out. They appear to be a better investment than other things, and they become fashionable, an investment fad.

Of course, the apples might indeed be a good investment if — and this is a big if — your timing is correct. You must buy at the right time, and sell at the right time. And it is possible. Some people earn handsome incomes by doing nothing but buying and selling at the right times. They know how to profit from the boom-and-bust cycle.

Unfortunately, many other people earn tickets to the poor house by trying to do that. Your timing must be extraordinary.

One of history's best examples of the boom-and-bust cycle is the Great Stock Market Crash of 1929. All during the late 1920's people had been pouring money into the stock market. Then the government stopped creating money, and the supply of new dollars dried up. The same people who stampeded into the stock market started stampeding out. In only a few days, thousands of rich people became poor.

A similar incident, one of the strangest, happened in Holland about 350 years ago. It was called tulipomania.

Thousands of the Dutch were looking for a get-rich-quick scheme and they discovered the idea of investing in tulips. There were so many people buying tulips and expecting to resell them for a profit, that the price of tulips went almost straight up. At one point someone paid $5200 for one tulip bulb.

Of course, after a few years the tulipomania stopped, and prices came back down to reasonable levels. People who sold out before the insanity ended made a fortune. But most of the investors lost a great deal.

If you don't want to be like the victims of 1929 or of tulipomania, either stay away from get-rich-quick fads, or be very careful. Learn everything there is to know about your investments. Become an expert about them, and remember that big rewards usually carry big risks. Above all, never trust anyone else to watch your investments for you — no one cares about you as much as you do, so no one is going to be as watchful as you are.

And, you'll need the courage of a river boat gambler, because that's the business you'll be in: gambling.

Speaking of business and investments, you might consider starting your own business. Many types of businesses require very little cash to get into. This might be the best investment you can make. Be your own boss. If you do it wisely, your risks will be lower and your rewards far greater than with any other kind of investment.

Most businesses and investment portfolios can be made almost immune to the effect of the inflation-recession "boom-and-bust" business cycle. In fact, when the right strategy is used, they can generate enormous profits from the cycle. The system is called Business Cycle Management or BCM. (After I finish this set of letters on economics I'll write you in depth about BCM[3]).

Consider starting a business. The economic turmoil is growing and a business is probably now the best way for a young person to get ahead. Good Luck!

Uncle Eric

---

[3] Contact Bluestocking Press, PO Box 1014-PC3, Placerville, CA 95667, and ask about the sequel to WHATEVER HAPPENED TO PENNY CANDY?

10

The Boom and Bust Cycle

Dear Chris,

With gold and silver eliminated from our money, no one is quite sure what is money and what isn't. Many definitions are used. One, M2, defines money as currency, checking accounts, travelers checks, savings accounts, money market mutual funds and certain transactions between banks.

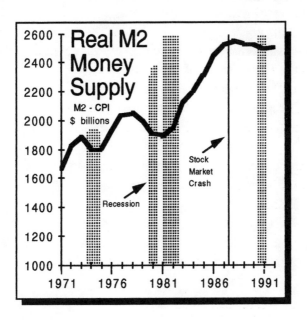

If we subtract consumer price increases from M2 we get the "real" M2 money supply.

Each time the government slows the creation of real M2, a recession hits.

The 1982 recession was the worst since the Great Depression. To end it, officials inflated the money supply heavily between 1983 and 1986. Some of this new money went into stocks causing the stock market to rise. This caught the attention of millions of investors. They climbed on the bandwagon, stocks became fashionable, a fad.

Much of the new money was channeled into the stock market causing an enormous boom; the market shot from 800 in 1982 to 2722 in 1987.

When inflation of M2 was slowed in 1987, the supply of new money to the stock market dried up. We got one of the worst stock market crashes in history, and eventually a recession.

Uncle Eric

11

How Much is a Trillion?

Dear Chris[4],

You said you've been studying the federal debt (the so-called national debt) and are having trouble understanding its size, $4 trillion, that's

$4,000,000,000,000.00

Frankly, I believe the only people able to understand the federal debt now are astronomers. I'm serious, the federal debt has become so huge that it can be grasped only by persons who are comfortable discussing the number of light years spanned by our galaxy. This is why so few politicians worry about the debt. They've made it so big that it is no longer *real* to them, it's just meaningless numbers. But I'll try to help you get a handle on it.

Do you consider $1 million to be a lot of money? Imagine what you could buy with it. Make a list.

Now visualize $1 million in $100 bills laid end-to-end. You'd need 20 minutes to walk the length of this line of cash, it's about one mile.

---

[4] This letter is derived from an article in the April 1992 issue of Richard Maybury's newsletter.

Walk a line of $100 bills the length of the federal debt and it would take you 137 years. This line of $100 bills would circle the earth 144 times.

If Columbus, when he stepped ashore in America, had immediately begun borrowing money at the rate of $10,000 per minute, by 1993 he would still not have borrowed the equivalent of today's federal debt.

Something happened in the early 1980s. Apparently officials made a deliberate decision to borrow without limit, to wallpaper the world with their bonds. (A bond is an IOU.)

How will they repay these bonds?

How will they pay the interest on them?

What do you think?

Uncle Eric

Cherish public credit. One method of preserving it is to use it as sparingly as possible.

George Washington
First President of the United States

During the 1980's, the federal government's uncontrolled tax-and-spend policy became an uncontrolled tax-and-borrow-and-spend policy.

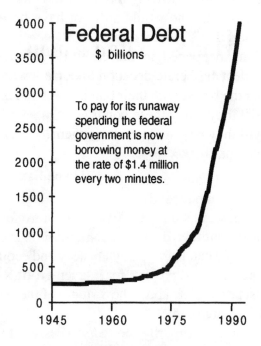

Federal Debt

$ billions

To pay for its runaway spending the federal government is now borrowing money at the rate of $1.4 million every two minutes.

Officials took 194 years to accumulate their first trillion dollars of debt and only five years to accumulate their second trillion. In 1990 they scored their third trillion, and in 1992 their fourth. Now they are working on their fifth.

Annual interest payments are roughly $1100 per person per year, which means the average family of four pays $4400 per year just for interest on the federal debt.Obviously this cannot go on forever. What do you think the government will do?

Remember, governments have no real wealth of their own, they have only what they have taken from others.

12

What's So Bad About
the Federal Debt?

Dear Chris[5],

"You certainly are pessimistic," said the talk show host who interviewed me recently.

Yes, I'm pessimistic about America's future for the next ten years or so, but this doesn't mean individuals cannot be exceptions. They can learn enough history and economics to see what's coming and prepare for it, even profit.

I'm most pessimistic about the fortunes of the young. For them good jobs are scarce.

Why? A job is primarily the *tools* necessary to produce what others want to buy. A man with a $50,000 hydraulic backhoe can dig far more ditches than one with a $20 shovel. He can earn much higher wages and do more for his family.

Where does money for tools come from? Savings. Someone saves the $50,000 and puts it in stocks, bonds or bank CDs where it is available for businesses to use. Businesses borrow this money, buy the equipment and hire workers.

---

[5] This article appeared in the August 1992 issue of Richard Maybury's newsletter.

If the $50,000 isn't saved, or if it is borrowed and spent by the government, it is not available to businesses. The backhoe isn't purchased and the worker is stuck with the $20 shovel and low wages.

In the U.S. today the average worker uses about $71,000 worth of tools. But the government's spending is now so much greater than its income that it is borrowing $1.4 million every two minutes. This soaks up money that should be going into stocks and so forth for tools to create jobs.

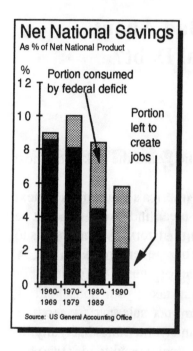

Divide $1.4 million by $71,000. The government's deficit is consuming 20 jobs every two minutes; it's wiping out 262,800 jobs per year.

And, this damage is from the *deficit* only. We cannot know how much savings is eaten directly by *taxes* but it's certainly a lot more. Savings are declining. I'm sure the government is now so large and powerful it is consuming more than a million jobs annually.

Former U.S. Treasury Secretary William Simon calls this "the great American seed corn banquet." When a farmer harvests a crop he saves a portion as seed to plant for next year's crop. If this seed is eaten...

We affluent members of the over-the-hill generations won't be hurt too badly but the young are absolutely dependent on a steady supply of new jobs, and our huge, voracious government is eating these jobs.

Uncle Eric

An Interesting Exercise

Until the 1970s, most families were able to improve their standard of living with only one adult working outside the home. In the 1970s, '80s and '90s, mothers and wives got paying jobs, usually on the assumption they were helping support their families.

Try this. Add up the total taxes your household pays—state and federal income tax, sales tax, property tax and any others you can find (remember that many taxes are "hidden taxes" that aren't easy to identify). Compare the total taxes paid with the total wages earned.

Chances are you'll find one spouse is supporting the household, and the other is supporting the government.

13

Summary

Dear Chris,

My next letter will be the last one, so I want to summarize what I've told you about inflations and recessions.

1. Inflation is an increase in the amount of money. When the amount of money goes up, the value goes down. When the value goes down, people need more of it. Rising prices are not inflation, they are a result of inflation. The wage/price spiral is a result, not a cause, of inflation.

2. Inflation causes business people to make mistakes. When the inflation stops, the business people see their mistakes and start making corrections. They must fire workers, and unemployment goes up.

3. If the inflation starts up again, the corrections stop and the workers go back to work. A recession has happened.

4. If the inflation does not start up again, the corrections are completed. Unemployment stays up for a longer time because the workers cannot go back to their old jobs, they must find new ones. That's a depression.

5. Inflation causes recessions and depressions. The only way to have no recessions or depressions is to never start inflating. Once inflation has started, there is no known way to avoid the results.

I hope one of the things my letters have taught you is that history is not just a collection of names, dates, wars and revolutions. History is a logical sequence of events. You don't need to be a professional historian to understand it, and once you do understand it you will be better able to cope with the events of today.

In my opinion, the quickest and easiest way to understand history is to study the history of money, especially gold and silver. That's because money is a mirror of civilization. Throughout history, whenever we find good, reliable non-inflated money, we almost always find a strong, healthy civilization. Whenever we find unreliable, inflated money we almost always find a civilization in decay.

The biggest and best example I know of is Europe's Dark Ages. During the Dark Ages, all of Europe was in a terrible, poverty stricken condition; we might call it the biggest and longest (about 500 A.D. to 1000 A.D.) depression in the history of mankind. A major reason why the Dark Ages lasted so long is that there was no money which was reliable enough to be widely accepted — the money of the Roman Empire had decayed along with the Empire. The lack of reliable money made production and trade very difficult, so people were unable to lift themselves above the poverty level.

It wasn't until good, reliable money like the thaler began to circulate that Europe came out of its Dark Ages.

Today, if you travel around the world you will find that the countries which have the best money, like Germany and Switzerland, also have the healthiest economies. Those countries are good places to live. The countries which have the worst money, like Chile, Mexico and Argentina, also have the weakest economies. I would not like to live there.

This brings up an interesting question. Does good money

create a healthy civilization or does a healthy civilization create good money? Which comes first, the chicken or the egg?

I believe TANSTAAFL comes first. I have noticed that whenever and wherever the money begins to turn rotten, someone, either voters or politicians or both, has forgotten that you can't get something for nothing.

When that happens, these people stop trying to produce what they need. They start looking for tricks and gimmicks — which usually means stealing or inflation — in order to get what they need.

On the other hand, whenever and wherever people respect the fact that we cannot have more unless we produce more, the money stays solid and the civilization stays healthy. That's because the specialization of labor which makes civilization possible can only happen when good reliable money exists.

In other words, don't believe the old saying about money being the root of all evil. On the contrary, money is the foundation of our whole world. If we respect that foundation and make it solid, there will be almost no limits to what we can accomplish.

When I say almost no limits, I am not exaggerating. Have you ever heard of the "German Miracle?" That "miracle" is living proof that we can accomplish almost anything if we make wise economic decisions.

At the end of World War II, Germany was in ruins, much of it had been bombed back into the Dark Ages. A great deal of the housing had been destroyed, millions of workers had been killed, and the lines of transportation and communication had been demolished. Entire cities had been leveled and whole industries had disappeared. The money was hyper-inflated so badly that it was worthless.

Wage/price controls, which had been started by the Nazis and rigidly enforced by the Gestapo during the war, and by the military governors after the war, had created a black market. But even the black market was unable to supply the people with enough food, clothing or other necessities.

People were reverting back to barter, and they were leaving the cities to go out into the countryside where they could forage for food. In some places the poverty and famine were so bad that the people had returned to the Stone Age.

As if all that trouble were not bad enough, Germany was overrun by immigrants, 8.5 million of them, who were fleeing from the countries which had been captured by the Russian government.

I once met a woman who was in Germany during that time, and she told me about some of the things that happened to her. The robberies, murders, poverty and famine were terrible, as bad as the war itself. Most of her family died, and she was very lucky to have survived.

No one knew how to solve Germany's problems; no one, that is, except a small group of economists led by a man named Ludwig Erhard. Erhard was able to persuade the people who were governing Germany that the wage/price and other controls must be lifted. He also convinced them that taxes must be lowered and inflation must be stopped.

Most controls were lifted, taxes were lowered dramatically, and a new, hard (non-inflated) currency, the Deutschmark, was introduced. Almost overnight things got better. People who had been stealing and killing began working, and people who had abandoned the cities came back. Everyone knew that their hard work would be rewarded with hard money and the things hard money would buy. An eyewitness said:

Shops filled up with goods from one day to the next; the factories began to work. On the eve of currency reform the Germans were aimlessly wandering about their towns in search of a few additional items of food. A day later they thought of nothing but producing them. One day apathy was mirrored in their faces while on the next a whole nation looked hopefully into the future.

Germany not only came out of the Dark Ages, but by 1960 the country had fully recovered. Today Germany is one of the world's most prosperous nations. In the short span of 20 years, the German people went from barbaric poverty and chaos to a very high standard of living, a low rate of inflation, and a low unemployment rate. They owe it almost entirely to Ludwig Erhard and his fellow economists.

Unfortunately the "German Miracle" was confined to Germany. Other countries, like Britain, did not follow Erhard's advice. Although they ended the war in much better shape than Germany and received as much help from other countries as Germany, they are today much worse off than Germany. They have far more inflation and unemployment, and their people do not live as well as the Germans. It's really a shame.

So what about our future? Next letter.

Uncle Eric

14

Where Do We Go from Here?

Dear Chris,

As I said before, no other inflation in history has been as widespread (almost world-wide) as this one. We don't know exactly what to expect, but we can make some guesses.

Unfortunately, so few people understand what is happening that things may not change for a long time. It is possible that we'll keep going down this same inflationary path until we have a runaway inflation. It could take many years, maybe decades, but that's the way it's going.

However, if enough people learn what is happening, we do have a good chance to get out of this without much damage.

I believe modern communication and transportation are swift enough to make the necessary corrections very fast and easy. If people order their governments to stop inflating, we might get through the depression very quickly, within a year or two.

The biggest hazard is impatience. If people get in a hurry, they may demand that the politicians interfere with the businesspeople's corrections. That's what happened in the 1930's and it made the Great Depression a very long one. It caused the wrong corrections; then the corrections had to be corrected. It was a mess. There were more unemployed people in 1940 than in 1931. That's how much good Franklin Roosevelt's "New Deal" did.

For instance, people asked Mr. Roosevelt to make employers stop firing workers. The President did. But some business people didn't have enough money to keep paying all their workers. Instead of only a few workers losing their jobs, the businesses went broke and many workers lost their jobs.

People also asked the government to prevent foreign businesses from selling goods in the U.S. (and people in other countries were asking their governments for the same favor). The government did what the people asked, so foreign companies could not sell their products. They had to fire workers, and the depression spread around the world, getting worse and worse.

Fortunately this is not the 1930's. We understand better what is happening now. If enough people can be taught what causes the "boom-and-bust" business cycle, then maybe we can stop it, at least for a while.

We can learn a lesson from ancient Greece. For many decades, voters in Athens elected only the politicians who would take an oath against debasing the money. The oath was taken every twelve months. It stopped the inflation and depressions, and Athens became a very rich city. Life was pleasant for many years.

In the Byzantine Empire, people were so afraid of inflation and depression that anyone who clipped coins had his hand cut off. It was cruel but it worked. For a time there was no inflation or depression. In fact, the Byzantine coin, the bezant, stayed valuable for a thousand years. It was probably the best money in history; people were glad to have it because they knew its value would not fall.

Before I finish writing, I want to share a lesson I've learned.

You'll notice a lot of people like to blame their enemies for the inflation and recessions. Republicans blame Democrats, labor blames management, Whites blame Blacks, poor people blame rich people, and so forth. As prices and unemployment go up, hatred spreads. A person starts hating people he's never even met.

Be careful you don't fall into this trap. It has destroyed a lot of people and a lot of countries. For example:

In some areas of Europe, the money lending, banking, and other financial work is done mostly by Jewish people. That's because Christians in these areas believe the Bible tells them not to do that kind of work. Therefore, in some towns, the only people who understand money are Jewish.

During World War I, when one of the German runaway inflations started, only a few Germans knew enough about money to know what would happen. They were mostly Jewish. Compared to everyone else they were wealthy.

When Hitler came to power, he made speeches about Jews being the only rich people in Germany. He said the Jews caused the Germans' troubles to get rich from it. That's how Hitler was able to start persecuting the Jews.

These kinds of things happen over and over again. The reason is that people think economics is too hard to understand.

Instead of learning what is happening and what to do about it, they just get mad. Then they start looking for revenge. They go on "witch hunts."

We haven't seen the last of inflations, recessions or depressions, so be sure you aren't part of any "witch hunts." Learn more about economics. I suggest you write The Foundation For Economic Education, Irvington-On-Hudson, New York, 10533. Tell them who you are, how you heard about them and that you'd like to learn more about economics.

Remember tanstaafl. "There Ain't No Such Things As A Free Lunch." And spread the word.

                              Uncle Eric

Appendix

Spreading the Word

Many readers of WHATEVER HAPPENED TO PENNY CANDY? purchase additional copies to distribute to friends. One way to do this is to go to your local bookstore and ask the clerk to order it from Bluestocking Press (SAN 667-2981), P.O. Box 1014, Dept. PC3, Placerville, CA 95667-1014, Phone: 800-959-8586, 916-621-1123. Fax: 916-642-9222. Let them know that Bluestocking Press is a participant of the Single Title Order Plan (STOP). Or, you can order WHATEVER HAPPENED TO PENNY CANDY? direct from Bluestocking Press by sending $9.95 U.S. for each copy ordered plus $3.00 shipping for the first book, and $0.75 for each additional book. Books shipped to a California address must include sales tax. Bulk discounts are available for quantity purchases.

Spreading the word in Canada

A Canadian supplement to WHATEVER HAPPENED TO PENNY CANDY? has been published by WT Educational Services (12563 Carrs Landing Road, Winfield, British Columbia, V4V 1A1). This supplement explains the differences between American and Canadian monetary and economic history so that Canadian readers can more easily apply the principles and economics found in WHATEVER HAPPENED TO PENNY CANDY? to their own country.

Please Write "Uncle Eric" With Your Ideas, Questions and Concerns

Watch for future books by Richard J. Maybury. One will be answers to questions from readers. Send your questions or comments to him in care of "Uncle Eric," Bluestocking Press, P.O. Box 1014, Dept. PC3, Placerville, CA 95667-1014. All letters become property of Bluestocking Press and may be published in whole or in part without payment to the writer. Please tell us if you want your name kept confidential. Topics can include, but are not limited to economics, government, history and law.

If your letter is published in a future "Uncle Eric" book or used in a future "Uncle Eric" audiocassette tape you will receive a free autographed copy of that book or tape.

This excerpt from The Long Winter shows the attitude early Americans had toward government and taxes.

Excerpted with permission from
THE LONG WINTER
by Laura Ingalls Wilder

Mr. Edwards admired the well-built, pleasant house and heartily enjoyed the good dinner. But he said he was going West with the train when it pulled out. Pa could not persuade him to stay longer.

"I'm aiming to go far West in the spring," he said. "This here country, it's too settled-up for me. The politicians are a-swarming in already, and ma'am if'n there's any worst pest than grasshoppers it surely is politicians. Why, they'll tax the lining out'n a man's pockets to keep up these here county-seat towns! I don't see nary use for a county, nohow. We all got along happy and content without 'em.

"Feller come along and taxed me last summer. Told me I got to put in every last least thing I had. So I put in Tom and Jerry, my horses, at fifty dollars apiece, and my own yoke, Buck and Bright, I put in at fifty, and my cow at thirty-five.

"'Is that all you got?' he says. Well, I told him I'd put in five children I reckoned was worth a dollar apiece.

"'Is that all?' he says. 'How about your wife?' he says.

"'By Mighty! I says to him. 'She says I don't own her and I don't aim to pay no taxes on her.' I says. And I didn't."

"Why, Mr. Edwards, it is news to us that you have a family." said Ma. "Mr. Ingalls said nothing of it."

"I didn't know it myself," Pa explained. "Anyway, Edwards, you don't have to pay taxes on your wife and children."

"He wanted a big tax list," said Mr. Edwards. "Politicians, they take a pleasure a-prying into a man's affairs and I aimed to please 'em. It makes no matter. I don't aim to pay taxes. I sold the relinquishment on my claim and in the spring when the collector comes around I'll be gone from there. Got no children and no wife, nohow."

Sign posted in Trade Store
at Sutter's Fort State Historic Park
Sacramento, California

Courtesy of the Sutter's Fort Living History Program. This document
represents composite information and is not original to the Fort.

Notice

Discounting of Currency

1. *All Paper Currency drawn upon State Banks and State Offices of Comptrollers will be discounted 45% Per Centum on Transactions. There will be no Exceptions.*

2A. *Mexican and British Bank Drafts will be Discounted 27% Per Centum on Transaction. All Bank Drafts on Pacific Coast Merchants, Banks,*

2B. *Lending Houses, and Ships Pursuers will be discounted 33% Per Centum on all Transactions.*

3. *All Bank Drafts and Letters of Credit or Exchange, on European Merchants, Banks, Lending Houses or Governmental Agencies doing Business on this Coast and redeemable in Silver or Gold will be discounted at 15% or Exchanged at a 20% Discount.*

4. *All Coinage will be Exchanged ar Accepted at Face Value minus 5% on Volume of Business Transactions. Banking of Funds on Sandwich Island Accounts Payable - 5% of Volume.*

Drafts and Warrants upon this establishment will be

1. *Accepted at Face Value for Trades - or - at 10% Discount for Exchange of Coin or Drafts of Letters of Credit.*

By Order of
John A. Sutter
Proprieter

January 14, 1846 George N. Loker
Chief Clerk

The value of the money was reduced according to the risk of accepting
it. Store owners preferred money that was likely to retain its value.

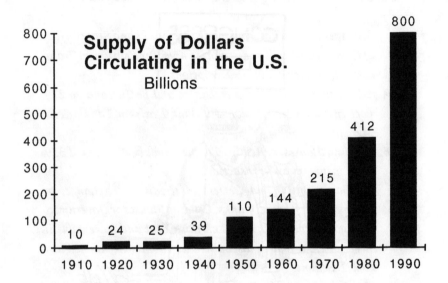

Supply of Dollars Circulating in the U.S.
Billings

800
700
600
500
400
300
200
100
0

1910: 10
1920: 24
1930: 25
1940: 39
1950: 110
1960: 144
1970: 215
1980: 412
1990: 800

M1 money supply.

THE WALL STREET JOURNAL

"I'm worried about 'zillion' rolling off my lips
the way 'billion' used to."

From *The Wall Street Journal* — Permission, Cartoon Features
Syndicate

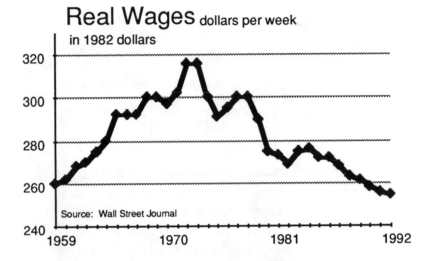

Real Wages dollars per week

in 1982 dollars

Source: Wall Street Journal

320 | 300 | 280 | 260 | 240

1959   1970   1981   1992

The "real" wage is the wage minus the effects of inflation. In the early 1970's real wages began falling. Being a wage-earner now means going steadily backwards.

Also, due to two-tier wage settlements during the 1980's, younger workers are frequently paid according to reduced wage scales. So, as wages fall, the young are hurt most.

"Average weekly earnings in real terms have been declining in recent years, and in the early months of 1990 they had receded to about the level of 30 years ago. If we had sustained rates of increase more in line with our history, or with what has been happening in Europe and Asia, today's average earnings from a week of work would be about 50% higher in real terms."

Paul W. McCracken, economist
Wall Street Journal

"Economists have traditionally concentrated on year-to-year fluctuations in output and had little to say about growth in the longer term. Questions such as why the rate of increase in GDP[6] per head in industrial economies slowed from an average of 3.5% in 1950-73 to 1.9% in 1973-1990 have been largely ignored. That is a shame. If growth had continued at its 1950-73 pace, real incomes today would be a third higher."

THE ECONOMIST, September 12th 1992

---

[6] GDP (Gross Domestic Product). Total of all the goods and services produced within the United States in a year.

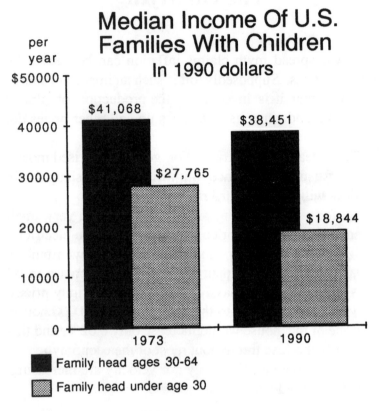

Median Income Of U.S.
Families With Children
In 1990 dollars

per
year

$50000

$41,068

$38,451

40000

$27,765

30000

$18,844

20000

10000

0

1973   1990

■ Family head ages 30-64

▨ Family head under age 30

Source: U.S. News & World Report

America is sliding backward. Since 1973, real incomes of young families have dropped more than 32%. This is due not so much to their own shortcomings, as to the disorganization of the economy caused by the government's inflation.

The Oil Myth

A widespread myth claims inflation can be caused by rising oil prices. Supposedly, oil is such an important source of energy that it is involved in the production of almost everything and when its price goes up, all other prices do, too.

This is really a half-truth. For goods comprised mostly of oil — plastics for instance — it's quite true. A sharp rise in oil prices will cause a sharp rise in plastic prices.

But for most goods the price of oil is only a very small percentage of the total price. For example, the electricity used by all the carpenters and other workmen who build a $200,000 house is less than $20.00. If an increase in oil prices were to cause a massive tripling of electricity prices, this would add only $40 to the price of the $200,000 house. The price of the house would increase only 0.02%, and this is typically the case throughout most of the economy.

If neither the money supply nor velocity are increasing, the overall price level cannot increase.

How to Invest in
Gold and Silver

Gold and silver are financial insurance not only against severe inflation but also against all other kinds of turmoil. For thousands of years, through wars, revolutions, depressions, famines — even the fall of the Roman Empire and the Dark Ages — gold and silver have always retained at least some of their value. No other investment has done this.

In other words, gold and silver are financial bedrock. They survive when nothing else does.

A good way to own gold and silver is in the form of bullion coins like the American Eagle or the Canadian Maple Leaf.

Resources

The Baseball Game. A classroom game for ages six to adult. Students buy and sell cardboard baseballs. Demonstrates how prices are determined by supply and demand. Available from the Academy for Economic Education, 125 Sovran Center, Richmond, VA 23277, (804) 643-0071.

Center for Business and Economic Education, Lubbock Christian University, 5601 West 19th Street, Lubbock, TX 79407. Sells a packaged business venture kit called "The Chocolate Factory" which gives kids a hands on experience of how a manufacturing business works. It may be used as a private ownership, partnership, or corporation. A stock certificate is enclosed to be photocopied for each student stockholder. The kit includes chocolate melts, molds, sticks and instructions. The purpose of the business is to make a profit. A kit costs $40 plus postage and contains enough inventory to produce approximately 130 chocolate suckers. If all 130 are sold at $.75 each, the operating profit will be $57.50. Stock dividends may be declared, or profits reinvested in inventory.

Durell Foundation Teaching Kit on Money and Banking, The George Edward Durell Foundation, P.O. Box 847, Berryville, VA 22611. Enlightening, in-depth presentation about money and banking. Excellent history of money. High school, college or adult. Important for investors and business managers, too. Highly recommended.

Junior Business Basics—for Kids, Achievement Basics, 800 S. Fenton Street, Lakewood, CO 80226. Teaches good business habits and some free-market economics through cassette tape stories and printed materials. Christian biblical emphasis on character building. Grade school and junior high school.

National Schools Committee for Economic Education, Inc. 86 Valley Road, P.O. Box 295, Cos Cob, Connecticut, 06807-0295, 203-869-1706. "Presents basic principles and values of the American economic system in simple, understandable language illustrated with the famous NSCEE cartoon characters.....The materials are supplementary and can be worked into any teaching plan in social studies, career, business or consumer education." Material appropriate for grades one through twelve and adult audiences. Excellent for teaching and learning about how the world works. Great for young and old alike, especially if you were baffled by college courses in economics. Outstanding emphasis on the fundamental connection between production and Constitutional law. Presentation is aimed at junior high school age group but information is enlightening to all ages.

The Foundation for Economic Education, Inc. " is a nonpolitical, nonprofit, educational institution. Its senior staff and numerous writers are students as well as teachers of the free market, private ownership, limited government rationale. Sample copies of the Foundation's monthly study journal, *The Freeman*, are available on request." FEE also has a series of articles oriented to children entitled *Fundamentals of Freedom,* and sponsors an annual student essay contest. Foundation for Economic Education, Inc. Irvington-on-Hudson, New York 10533.

The Independent Institute is a free market research and educational organization. Books, magazine and newsletter. Highly recommended. The Independent Institute, 134 98th Avenue, Oakland, CA 94603, 415-632-1366.

Cassettes, Games and Software

Jeffrey Norton Publishers, audio cassettes on free market subjects (i.e. Milton Friedman, Murray Rothbard, and Ludwig von Mises), Suite RCC-103, On-The-Green, 96 Broad Street, Guilford, CT 06437, 1-800-243-1234.

Knowledge Products Audio Cassettes. Interesting and well produced stories about great economists and the importance of their ideas to our businesses, careers and investments. Narrated by Louis Rukeyser, host of television's *Wall Street Week*. The cassettes about Austrian economics are especially important *(The Austrian Case for Free Market Process* by Ludwig von Mises and Friedrich Hayek; *Early Austrian Economics* by Carl Menger, Eugen von Bohm-Bawerk, and other pioneers). Highly recommended. High school, college or adult. Knowledge Products, 1717 Elm Hill Pike, Suite A4, P.O. Box 305151, Nashville, TN 37230, (800) 876-4332.

Lemonade Stand (for MacIntosh computers), Nordic Software, 3939 N. 48th St., Lincoln, NE 68504, 800-228-0417. Simulation of a lemonade stand. You select the amount of glasses to be sold, amount of signs you wish to buy for advertising. Profits based on your decisions. Weather changes, competitors interfere.

Made for Trade, Aristoplay Ltd., P.O. Box 7028, Ann Arbor, MI 48107 (313) 995-4353 for ages 8 through Adult. Board game in the free enterprise spirit.

Settling America (for Apple II family, IBM PC and Pcjr.), World Book Publishing, 525 West Monroe, Station 20, Chicago, IL 60606, 800-323-6366. Simulation of life in a free market economy (1789-1793) in the Ohio Valley.

Financial Newsletters

These financial newsletter writers are familiar with the economic forces described in *Whatever Happened to Penny Candy?* and they take these forces into account when making recommendations.

Larry Abraham, INSIDER REPORT, P.O. Box 84903, Phoenix, AZ 85071

Joseph Bradley, INVESTOR'S HOTLINE, 10616 Beaver Dam Rd., Hunt Valley, MD 21030

Harry Browne, HARRY BROWNE'S SPECIAL REPORTS, P.O. Box 5586, Austin, TX 78763

Douglas Casey, CRISIS INVESTING, P.O. Box 5195, Helena, MT 59604

Adrian Day, INVESTMENT ANALYST, P.O. Box 6644, Annapolis, MD 21401

R.E. McMaster, THE REAPER, Box 84901, Phoenix, AZ 85071

Richard J. Maybury, RICHARD MAYBURY'S U.S. & WORLD EARLY WARNING REPORT FOR INVESTORS, P.O. Box 1616-CP3, Rocklin, CA 95677

Ron Paul, THE RON PAUL INVESTMENT LETTER, 1120 NASA Blvd. #104, Houston, TX 77058

Jack Pugsley, JOHN PUGSLEY'S JOURNAL, P.O. Box 462890, Escondido, CA 92046

Daniel Rosenthal, SILVER & GOLD REPORT, P.O. Box 510, Bethel, CT 06801

Mark Skousen, FORECASTS & STRATEGIES, P.O. Box 2488, Winter Park, FL 32790

Mail-Order Book Stores

Sources of information about inflation, business cycles, economics and related subjects for children and adults.

Bluestocking Press Catalog, P.O. Box 1014, Dept. PC3, Placerville, CA 95667. Telephone (800) 959-8586 (for orders); (916) 621-1123 (for customer service)

Foundation for Economic Education, Irvington-on-Hudson, NY 10533

Henry-Madison Research, Box 1616-CP3, Rocklin, CA 95677

Laissez Faire Books, 942 Howard Street, San Francisco, CA 94103, (800) 326-0996

Liberty Tree Network, 134 98th Avenue, Oakland, CA 94603. Telephone (800) 927-8733 for orders; (415) 568-6047 for customer service; FAX: (415) 568-6040

NSCEE'S *Materials for Teaching Economic Principles,* 86 Valley Road, P.O. Box 295, Cos Cob, CT 06807

the Liberator, Advocates for Self-Government, Inc. 1115 Sundial Circle, Birmingham, AL 35215

Distilled Wisdom

Federal Debt

"The question, whether one generation of men has a right to bind another, seems never to have been started. ... [I believe] no generation can contract debts greater than may be paid during the course of its own existence. ... The conclusion then, is, that neither the representatives of a nation, nor the whole nation itself assembled, can validly engage debts beyond what they may pay in their own time."

Thomas Jefferson, 1743-1826
Author, Declaration of Independence

"If the debt should once more be swelled to a formidable size, its entire discharge will be despaired of, and we shall be committed to the English career of debt, corruption and rottenness, closing with revolution."

Thomas Jefferson

"Cherish public credit. One method of preserving it is to use it as sparingly as possible." **George Washington**
First President of the United States

"Avoiding likewise the accumulation of debt, not only by shunning occasions of expense, but by vigorous exertions in time of peace to discharge debts which unavoidable wars may have occasioned, not ungenerously throwing upon posterity the burden which we ourselves ought to bear."

George Washington

Taxes & Government Spending

"Now what liberty can there be where property is taken without consent?"   **Samuel Adams, 1722-1803**
American Revolutionary and
Leader of Boston Tea Party

"The public money of this country is the toil and labor of the people, who are under many uncommon difficulties and distresses at this time, so that all reasonable frugality ought to be observed."   **John Adams, 1735-1826**
American Revolutionary and
2nd President of the United States

"If we run into such [government] debts, as that we must be taxed in our meat and in our drink, in our necessaries and our comforts, in our labors and our amusements, for our callings and our creeds, as the people of England are, our people, like them, must come to labor sixteen hours in the twenty-four, give the earnings of fifteen of these to the government for their debts and daily expenses, and the sixteenth being insufficient to afford us bread, we must live, as they now do, on oatmeal and potatoes, have no time to think, no means of calling the mismanagers to account; but be glad to obtain subsistence by hiring ourselves to rivet their chains on the necks of our fellow-sufferers."   **Thomas Jefferson**

"We must then tell you that we will never submit to be hewers of wood or drawers of water for any ministry or nation in the world."   **John Jay, 1745-1829**
American Revolutionary and
co-author of *The Federalist Papers*

Inflation & Paper Money

"The loss which America has sustained since the peace, from the pestilent effects of paper money on the necessary confidence between man and man, on the necessary confidence in the public councils, on the industry and morals of the people, and on the character of republican government, constitutes an enormous debt against the states chargeable with this unadvised measure."
James Madison, 1751-1836
Architect of U.S. Constitution

"That paper money has some advantages, is admitted. But that its abuses also are inevitable, and, by breaking up the measure of value, makes a lottery of all private property, cannot be denied. Shall we ever be able to put a constitutional veto on it?"
Thomas Jefferson

"You have to choose (as a voter) between trusting the natural stablity of gold and the honesty and intelligence of members of the government. And with due respect for these gentlemen, I advise you, as long as the capitalist system lasts, to vote for gold."
George Bernard Shaw, 1856-1950
Playwright & novelist

"The best way to destroy the capitalist system is to debase the currency."
Nikolai Lenin, 1870-1924
Socialist founder of the Soviet Union

"There is no subtler, or surer means of overturning the existing basis of society than to debase the currency. The process engages all the hidden forces of economic law on the side of destruction, and does it in a manner which only one man in a million is able to diagnose."
John Maynard Keynes
1883-1946, Economist

"A wagon-load of money will scarcely purchase a wagon-load of provisions."   **George Washington**

Commerce and Wealth

"In transactions of trade it is not to be supposed that, as in gaming, what one party gains the other must necessarily lose. The gain to each may be equal. If A has more corn than he can consume, but wants cattle; and B has more cattle, but wants corn; exchange is gain to each; thereby the common stock of comforts in life is increased."

Benjamin Franklin, 1706-1790
Signer, *Declaration of Independence*

"The statesman who should attempt to direct private people in what manner they ought to employ their capitals would not only load himself with a most unnecessary attention, but assume an authority which could safely be trusted, not only to no single person, but to no council or senate whatever, and which would nowhere be so dangerous as in the hands of a man who had folly and presumption enough to fancy himself fit to exercise it."   **Adam Smith, 1723-1790**
Economist

"Property is the fruit of labor; property is desirable; is a positive good in the world. That some should be rich shows that others may become rich, and hence is just encouragement to industry and enterprise. Let not him who is houseless pull down the house of another, but let him work diligently to build one for himself, thus by example assuring that his own shall be safe from violence when built."

Abraham Lincoln, 1809-1865
16th President of the United States

Political Power and Government

"Government is not reason, it is not eloquence; it is force! Like fire, it is a dangerous servant and a fearful master."

George Washington

"The people never give up their liberties but under some delusion."
Edmund Burke, 1729-1797
British statesman

"Rightful liberty is unobstructed action according to our will within limits drawn around us by the equal rights of others. I do not add 'within the limits of the law,' because law is often but the tyrant's will, and always so when it violates the rights of the individual."
Thomas Jefferson

"America is great because America is good. When America ceases to be good, America will cease to be great."
Alexis de Tocqueville, 1805-1859
Sociologist

"I am more and more convinced that man is a dangerous creature; and that power, whether vested in many or a few, is ever grasping, and, like the grave, cries 'Give, give."
Abigail Adams, 1744-1818
Wife of President John Adams

"It is strangely absurd to suppose that a million human beings collected together are not under the same moral laws which bind each of them separately."
Thomas Jefferson

"Sometimes it is said that man cannot be trusted with the government of himself. Can he, then, be trusted with the government of others?"
Thomas Jefferson

"In politics we are most ruthless when we are trying to be altruistic."   **Anonymous**

"There are severe limits to the good that the government can do for the economy, but there are almost no limits to the harm it can do."   **Milton Friedman, 1912-**
Nobel laureate

"Never blame a legislative body for not doing something. When they do nothing, that don't hurt nobody. When they do something they can be dangerous."
Will Rogers, 1879-1935
Humorist and columnist

"He has erected a multitude of new offices, and sent hither swarms of officers to harass our people, and eat out their substance."   *Declaration of Independence,* **1776**

"The history of liberty is a history of limitation of government power, not the increase of it."
Woodrow Wilson, 1856-1924
28th President of the United States

"The pleasure of governing must certainly be exquisite, if we may judge from the vast numbers who are eager to be concerned with it."   **Voltaire, 1694-1778**
French writer

"Every time government attempts to handle our affairs, it costs more and the results are worse than if we had handled them ourselves."   **Benjamin Constant, 1833-1891**
Brazilian statesman

Education

"Men give me some credit for genius. All the genius I have lies in this: When I have a subject in hand, I study it profoundly. Day and night it is before me. I explore it in all its bearings. My mind becomes pervaded with it. Then the effort which I make, the people are pleased to call the fruit of genius. It is the fruit of labor and thought."

Alexander Hamilton, 1757-1804
First U.S. Treasury Secretary

"If I have ever made any valuable discoveries, it has been owing more to patient attention, than to any other talent."

Sir Isaac Newton, 1642-1727
Mathematician

"Five per cent of the people think; ten per cent of the people think they think; and the other eighty-five per cent would rather die than think." **Thomas Edison, 1847-1931**
Inventor

Bibliography
and Recommended Reading

If you would like to have a better understanding of the economic events which affect your life, this list is a good place to start. I suggest you begin with *Economics in One Lesson, The Incredible Bread Machine, I Pencil* and *Free Market Economics: A Basic Reader.* Then go on to *Atlas Shrugged.* Thereafter you should have no trouble selecting other works.

Many of these books and articles are more than a decade old. Notice how accurate the predictions have been. There isn't much happening today that was not foreseen. History repeats.

Contact your librarian for locating out-of-print books.

Brown, Susan Love, et al. *The Incredible Bread Machine.* Written by and for college students. A clear, concise, entertaining look at economic issues. Don't miss it. Currently out of print. Inquire from W.R.I. Education, Box 9359, San Diego, CA 92169-0359. For ages 13 and up.

Browne, Harry. *How you Can Profit from the Coming Devaluation.* Don't let the sensationalistic ballyhoo on the cover scare you. The investment advice is outdated, but the first 100 pages contain an outstanding explanation of inflation, the business cycle, and the way the banks and Federal Reserve System work. Published by Avon Books, New York, NY. For ages 14 and up.

Browne, Harry. *Why the Best-Laid Investment Plans Usually Go Wrong.* Explains why investment plans rarely live up to their promises and how you can find safety and profit without having to rely on investment-market fortune-tellers. Published by William Morrow & Co., NY 1987. For ages 16 and up.

Burke, James. *Connections.* The book and TV series are excellent introductions to economic history and entertaining. Notice that the parts of the world that brought forth the most advancement and improvement were those that contained the most liberty. Published by Little, Brown & Co., Boston, 1978. For ages 13 and up.

Clark, Red G. and Rimanoczy, Richard S. *How We Live.* Published by American Economic Foundation, 1976, American Economic Foundation, c/o Mr. Homer W. Giles, 1215 Terminal Tower, Cleveland, OH 44113. (Also available through Bluestocking Press/Educational Spectrums Catalog). For ages 13 and up.

Economist, The. Best single source of news and analysis of the world economy. Weekly magazine. P.O. Box 58524, Boulder, CO, 80322. For ages 18 and up.

Greaves, Bettina B. *Free Market Economics: A Basic Reader.* Each of the eighty-one readings compiled by Bettina B. Greaves was "chosen to help explain or illustrate some aspect of the theory of free market economics." (from the author's Preface). This compilation can be read as an independent book but was designed to accompany and supplement *Free Market Economics: A Syllabus.* Mrs. Greaves studied for many years with the leading spokesman of the Austrian School of Economics - Ludwig von

Mises. Published by The Foundation for Economic Education, Inc., Irvington-on-Hudson, NY 10533. (Also available from Bluestocking Press/Educational Spectrums Catalog.) For ages 13 and up.

Greaves, Bettina B. *Free Market Economics: A Syllabus.* Written by Mrs. Greaves to answer the demand for a free market economics text to help teachers present free market ideas in the classroom. "It is my hope that in this Syllabus I have interpreted and 'translated' into simpler terms the profound economic theories set forth by Mises and his fellow 'Austrian' economists so that they may reach a new audience of teachers and, through them, young people on whom depend the prospects of freedom in the future." (from the author's Preface). Published by The Foundation for Economic Education, Inc., Irvington-on-Hudson, NY 10533. (Also available from Bluestocking Press/Educational Spectrums Catalog.) For ages 13 and up.

Hailey, Arthur. *The Moneychangers.* A novel about counterfeiting, money and banking. Published by Dell. For ages 16 and up.

Hazlitt, Henry, *Economics in One Lesson.* One of the best books on economics ever written. Very clearly and concisely exposes many cliches and fallacies. A good way to begin learning about economics. Published by Crown, ISBN 0-517-54823-2. (Also available from Bluestocking Press/Educational Spectrums Catalog.) For ages 14 and up.

Hazlitt, Henry. *The Inflation Crisis and How to Resolve It.* (formerly *What You Should Know About Inflation*). Describes the causes and effects of inflation. Written with Hazlitt's usual clarity. For order information contact The Foundation for Economic Education, Inc., Irvington-on-Hudson, NY 10533. For ages 16 and up.

Hess, Karl, *Capitalism for Kids: Growing Up to Be Your Own Boss.* Encourages children to become entrepreneurs. For ages 12 and up. Special section on education addressed to parents. Extensive directory. Published by Enterprise Publishing, Wilmington, DE, 1987. (Also available through Bluestocking Press/Educational Spectrums Catalog). For ages 9 and up.

Hoppe, Donald. *How to Invest in Gold Coins.* The first half of the book is an interesting history of money, from ancient civilizations until today. Published by Arco Publishing Co., New York, NY. Out of Print. For ages 15 and up.

LeFevre, Robert. *Lift her up, tenderly.* Economics converted into a story about a growing young girl of twelve-years old. Designed expecially for parents and young people. Available through Lois LeFevre, 27852 Cummins Dr., Laguna Niguel, CA 92677. For ages 12 and up.

Lockman, Vic, *Biblical Economics in Comics.* Using cartoon illustrations, this book presents an amazingly detailed and well thought out Christian explanation of the connection between Biblical principles and free-markets. Not for the faint-hearted, it forces the reader to choose between his government's law and his God's law. High School and adult readers. Published by Vic Lockman, 9921 Carmel Mountain Road, Suite 325, San Diego, CA 92129. For ages 9 and up.

Maidenberg, H. J. "Argentine Dilemma." *New York Times*. April 11, 1971. Describes inflationary events in Argentina. A preview of America's future? For ages 16 and up.

Maybury, Richard J. *How You Can Find the Best Investment Advice,* 40-page special report. The trade secrets of investment advisors, newsletters and brokers. A checklist of 12 important questions you should ask, rules of thumb, warning signs, profitability, risks vs. rewards, pitfalls, rip-offs, predictions, more. Published by Henry-Madison Research, Box 1616-CP3, Rocklin, CA 95677. For Adults.

Mises, Ludwig von. *Planned Chaos*. Compares Socialism, Fascism, Communism, and Welfare Statism. Mises is one of the greatest. Published by Foundation for Economic Education, Irvington-on-Hudson, NY. For ages 16 and up.

Peterson, Jean Ross. *It Doesn't Grow on Trees*. "Money doesn't (grow on trees) and don't let your children think it does.... This book will help." Betterway Publications, Box 219, Crozet, VA 22932, 1988 (also available through Bluestocking Press/Educational Spectrums Catalog). For Parents.

Peterson, William H. "The Sad Saga of Diocletian." *Wall*

Street Journal. October 3, 1973, p. 20. Inflation and wage/price controls in the Roman Empire. Excellent history. For ages 16 and up.

Rand, Ayn. *Atlas Shrugged.* A novel written three decades ago, used Austrian economics to predict economic events of today. Ms. Rand's description of the collapsing railroads is so accurate that you'll think she was psychic. Published by New American Library, New York, NY. For ages 16 and up.

Read, Leonard. "I, Pencil." *The Freeman Magazine.* December 1958. A classic. An outstanding description of the free market's method of allocating resources. Put this at the top of your list. Available from the Foundation for Economic Education, Irvington-on-Hudson, NY. For ages 12 and up.

Reason Foundation, *Econ Update* (September through May, monthly). For high school economics classes and college students, and specifically targeted at students who participate in high school speech and debate. For information write Econ Update, c/o Reason Foundation, 2716 Ocean Park Blvd., Ste. 1062, Santa Monica, CA 90405. For ages 14 and up.

Reason. Many excellent articles on economics. Magazine published by Reason Foundation, 2716 Ocean Park Blvd., Ste. 1062, Santa Monica, CA 90405. For ages 15 and up.

Riehm, Sarah L., *The Teenage Entrepreneur's Guide: 50 money-making business ideas,* 2nd edition. Can't say enough good about this book. Every parent and child should read it cover to cover. A great companion to *Capitalism for Kids*. Shows how to earn money by starting your own business. Instructions for both sides of each business — production and marketing. I wish I'd had this book when I was a teenager. Ages 10 and up. Published by Surrey Books, 230 E. Ohio Street, Suite 120, Chicago, IL 60611. (Also available from Bluestocking Press/ Educational Spectrums Catalog.) For ages 13 and up.

Rothbard, Murray N. *America's Great Depression*. A heavily documented textbook which details the 1920's inflation and 1930's depression. Available from LibertyTree, 134 98th Ave. Oakland, CA 94603. For ages 17 and up.

Sadler, Marilyn, *Ump's Fwat*. A clever and entertaining way of showing how a business evolves and how its profits create jobs and useful products. Age 10 (if the teacher is sharp) and up. Available from the Academy for Economic Education, 125 Sovran Center, Richmond, VA 23277, (804) 643-0071. For ages 7 and up.

Schwartz, David M., *If You Made a Million* and *How Much Is a Million*. Written and beautifully illustrated for young children but probably revealing to many adults. Helps you grasp the size of a million, billion and trillion. Makes the enormity of the government's debt more understandable — and frightening. Both are published by Lothrop, Lee & Shepard Books, New York. (*How Much Is a Million* is also available through Bluestocking Press/Educational Spectrums Catalog). For ages 7 and up.

Skousen, Mark, *Economics on Trial*. Analyzes current top ten economic textbooks and shows the fallacies on which they are based. Appropriate for high school level and above. Published by Business One Irwin, Homewood, IL. For ages 16 and up.

Skousen, Mark, *What Every Investor Should Know About Austrian Economics and the Hard-Money Movement* is a monograph published by the Mises Institute (Auburn University, Auburn, Alabama 36849). It introduces the importance of gold and other "hard" investments, and advisory services relating to them. For ages 16 and up.

The Basic Investor's Library series. Each small book is a short, easy course in some aspect of investing. This is mostly the "nuts and bolts" technical side, not economics. Great for learning the language of Wall Street. Essential for all investors. High school and adult. Published by Chelsea House Publishers, New York. For ages 14 and up.

Glossary

The meaning of economic terms varies according to the viewpoint of the person using them. This glossary contains definitions which the author believes would generally agree with the Austrian school of economics.

BANKNOTE. Today, paper money. Originally, an IOU from a bank, usually for gold or silver.

BASE METAL. A non-precious metal like copper or nickle.

BLACK MARKET. Producing, buying or selling something against the wishes of the government. Example: Liquor was a black market product during the "Prohibition Era."

BUSINESS. Production and trade. Also, an organization which produces and/or trades.

BUSINESS CYCLE. The boom/bust cycle. Prosperity followed by recession followed by prosperity followed by recession, and so forth.

CIRCULATION. The use or trading of money.

CLAD COIN. A sandwich coin. A coin made of layers of different metals.

CLIPPING COINS. Shaving the edges of a coin in order to get some of the precious metal from the coin.

COIN. A wafer or disk of precious metal. True coins usually have three markings; weight, fineness and name of mint.

COUNTERFEIT. Fake, phony.

CURRENCY. Money.

DEBASING. Reducing the value of a coin by reducing the amount of precious metal in it.

DEFLATION. A decrease in the amount of money. Usually causes depression and falling prices.

DENARIUS. A Roman coin originally made of 94 percent silver.

DEPRESSION. The correction period following an inflation. Usually includes a lot of business failures and unemployment.

DOUBLE-DIGIT INFLATION. Price increases rising at 10 to 99 percent per year due to inflation.

ECONOMICS. The study of the production and distribution of wealth.

ECONOMIST. A person who studies the production and distribution of wealth.

EXCHANGE. Trade.

FEDERAL RESERVE NOTE. A slip of paper issued by

the U.S. government, used as money, backed by a legal tender law.

FIAT MONEY. Legal tender money.

FINENESS. Purity of a precious metal. For instance if a coin is 900 fine gold, then it is 90 percent gold.

GRESHAM'S LAW. A law of economics; says bad money drives good money out of circulation. People hoard good money and trade with legally overvalued money.

HALLMARK. The mint-mark of a coin. Tells who made the coin. Like a trademark.

HARD MONEY. Non-inflated money, usually a commodity money such as gold or silver.

INFLATION. An increase in the amount of money. Causes the money to lose value, so prices rise.

LAW OF ECONOMICS. A fact of life which deals with production and distribution of wealth. You cannot change it, and it applies all over the world.

LEGAL TENDER LAW. A law which provides for the punishment of anyone who refuses to accept the legal tender money.

LEGAL TENDER MONEY. A legal medium of payment. Mint - A factory which makes coins or other money.

MONEY. The most easily traded thing in a society. Economists call it the most liquid commodity.

PRECIOUS METAL. A valuable metal like gold, platinum, or silver.

PRICE. What a person wants in trade for what he has.

PUBLIC WORKS. Government construction projects, like roads, dams, bridges.

RECESSION. The beginning of a depression which never went all the way.

REEDING. The notches on the edge of a coin.

REVOLUTION. Overthrowing a government, usually by force.

RUNAWAY INFLATION. A hyperinflation. Prices rising rapidly, every few hours.

SOFT MONEY. Inflated money. Usually legal tender.

STAGFLATION. A combination of too much unemployment and too much inflation, both occurring at the same time.

SUBSIDY. A government program for giving tax money away, usually to rich people or large companies. Welfare.

TANSTAAFL. (Sounds like tans-t-awful) "There Ain't No Such Thing As A Free Lunch." A popular expression during the Great Depression. Means that almost nothing is free, someone must pay for it. Tanstaafl is a law of economics.

TAX. The way governments get money. To tax means to take money away from someone, by force if necessary, even if he thinks what he is getting in return has little or no value.

TOKEN. A disk of base metal which can be used as a substitute for a coin.

VELOCITY. The speed at which money changes hands.

WAGE. The money a person gets for his work.

WEALTH. The goods and services people produce or convert to their use.

WELFARE. A government program for giving away money or goods, usually to poor people. A subsidy.

WITHDRAWALS. The painful process of getting un-hooked. Example: a depression is the withdrawal from inflation.

About
Richard J. Maybury
"Uncle Eric"

Richard J. Maybury, also known as "Uncle Eric," is the former Global Affairs editor of Moneyworld, and widely regarded as one of the top free-market writers in America. His articles have appeared in the Wall Street Journal, USA Today and other major publications.

President of Henry-Madison Research, he has been a consultant to business firms in the U.S. and Europe.

His books have been endorsed by top business leaders including former U.S. Treasury Secretary William Simon, and he has been interviewed on more than 200 radio and TV shows across America.

Mr. Maybury has authored several books in the "Uncle Eric" series and writes an investment newsletter.

He has been around the world, and visited 48 states and 23 countries.

He is a teacher for all ages.

Educators and Parents

This book (WHATEVER HAPPENED TO PENNY CANDY?) has been endorsed by educators, authors, and government officials for its unique contribution to the education of consumers from childhood to adulthood.

PTA Today

Easily Adapted for Classroom Use

WHATEVER HAPPENED TO PENNY CANDY? is easily adapted to classroom use. It is clear and interesting for students and is designed to foster critical thinking skills. It can be used in the following classes: economics, business, finance, consumer education, careers, current affairs and history. PENNY CANDY is an excellent springboard for discussion

Teacher Support Material Available

Teacher Support Material is available for a nominal fee and includes: A Note to Teachers, quiz, short answer essay questions, multiple choice questions, questions for discussion and activities (which were designed to show students how economic forces directly affect their daily lives). The Quiz and Short Answer Essay Questions are copyright free and ready to be reproduced on a copy machine.

Teacher Support Material ....$1.50 postpaid

Order from: Bluestocking Press, Box 1014
Dept. PC3, Placerville, CA 95667

INDEX

Henry-Madison Research

Richard Maybury writes an investment newsletter about stocks, geopolitics, economics, bonds, currencies, real estate, interest rates, precious metals and more. Much analysis is based on the connection between law and economics. Mr. Maybury gives special attention to events in the former USSR and Mideast, as well as in the U.S.

For a sample copy of Mr. Maybury's newsletter that gives you his latest thinking on important matters that affect you and your money send $5.00 to Henry-Madison Research, Box 1616-CP3, Rocklin, CA 95677.

For information about Mr. Maybury's lengthy special research reports send a self-addressed stamped business-size envelope to Henry-Madison Research, Box 1616-CP3, Rocklin, CA 95677.

" Uncle Eric" Writes Again

In his second "Uncle Eric" book, Richard Maybury answers the question:

Whatever Happened to Justice?

Economic problems are only symptoms, the cause is law. Inflation, recessions, business failures, unemployment and poverty are caused fundamentally by corruption of America's legal system.

The legal system we have today is not the one America's founders intended.

To learn more read Richard Maybury's WHATEVER HAPPENED TO JUSTICE? Besides defining the problem, Mr. Maybury offers practical solutions that can be applied at home, at school and in business.

From the International World of Economics

"This is a wonderfully readable and interesting book about the legal principles which undergird a free society. Richard Maybury challenges the reader to explore the inextricable connections between law and economics, and between economic and political liberty. I can think of no more important subject, and I highly recommend this lucid and thoughtful volume."

—William E. Simon
Former U.S. Treasury Secretary
and President, John M. Olin Foundation

From Congress

"Richard Maybury's *Whatever Happened to Justice?* is critical reading for all Americans. If our economic and political downfall is to be avoided, we must expose an entire generation of Americans to the ideas found in this wonderful book."

—Ron Paul, former member of Congress

From the World of Education

"There is a naked clarity to Maybury's thought that washes over the reader like cleansing rain. His examination of the dynamics of common law is brilliant. As a teacher for all ages, Mr. Maybury is a virtuoso. Bravo!"

—**John Taylor Gatto**
former New York State Teacher of the Year
author of DUMBING US DOWN

From the World of Homeschooling

"The author of WHATEVER HAPPENED TO PENNY CANDY? has done even better with WHATEVER HAPPENED TO JUSTICE? Maybury has a gift for translating what sounds like tedious information into very personalized examples. He follows the PENNY CANDY format, where Uncle Eric is writing to...Chris. Each letter is reasonably brief, so students will not be overwhelmed with too much information at once. Use this book as a supplement to American History or government studies. It will not take much time to read through, although it might generate lengthy discussions. No matter what else you use, this book is a must! Highly recommended for reading and discussion."

—**Cathy Duffy, Author**
CHRISTIAN HOME EDUCATORS' CURRICULUM MANUAL

From Authors

"We are drowning in an ocean of crazy laws and litigation. This book is a life preserver, a reminder of the fundamental rules which are needed for a free society."

—**Karl Hess**
author of CAPITALISM FOR KIDS
former U.S. Presidential speechwriter
former Associate Editor of NEWSWEEK

WHATEVER HAPPENED TO JUSTICE? Copyright, 1993, 256 pages, softcover, published by Bluestocking Press, P.O. Box 1014, Dept. PC3, Placerville, CA, 95667, (916) 621-1123. $14.95 U.S. (orders shipped to California, add sales tax), plus $3.00 shipping.

Bluestocking Press

"Uncle Eric" Books byRichard J. Maybury

UNCLE ERIC" TALKS ABOUT PERSONAL, CAREER & FINANCIAL SECURITY. . $ 7.95

WHATEVER HAPPENED TO PENNY CANDY? . . . . $ 9.95

PENNY CANDY TEACHER SUPPORT MATERIAL . . . . $ 0.95

WHATEVER HAPPENED TO JUSTICE? $14.95

ARE YOU LIBERAL? CONSERVATIVE? OR CONFUSED? . . . . $ 9.95

ANCIENT ROME: HOW IT AFFECTS YOUR TODAY . . . . $ 8.95

EVALUATING BOOKS: WHAT WOULD THOMAS JEFFERSON

        THINK ABOUT THIS? . . . . $ 8.95

Uncle Eric's Model (includes seven items above—save 10%) . . $55.95

Forthcoming title: Sequel to WHATEVER HAPPENED TO PENNY CANDY?...Query

Reprints

AGREEMENT BETWEEN PARENT & CHILD. . . . . $2.50 postpaid

AGREEMENT BETWEEN TEACHER & STUDENT. . . . . $2.50 postpaid

JONATHAN MAYHEW SERMON / JOHN ADAMS EXPLANATION OF

        THE AMERICAN REVOLUTION. $4.95

Other Bluestocking Press Titles

HOW TO STOCK A HOME LIBRARY INEXPENSIVELY. $14.95

THE HOME SCHOOL MARKET GUIDE . . . . $130.00 postpaid

Order information: Order any of the above from Bluestocking Press (see address below). Payable in U.S. funds. Prices subject to change without notice. If not postpaid, add shipping/handling: $2.50 (U.S.) or $3.50 (Foreign orders, surface) for the first book; add $0.75 for each add'l book. California residents add sales tax.

Also available

Bluestocking Press Resource Guide & Catalog . . . $3.00 within U.S.

The Bluestocking Press Resource Guide and Catalog lists over 1000 items with a concentration in American History, economics and law. It also includes sections on entrepreneurship, writing, critical thinking, math and classical music. This is a preK through adult level resource guide and catalog; history is arranged chronologically. It includes history products as follows: Fiction, nonfiction, primary source material, historical documents, facsimile newspapers, historical music, historical toy-making kits, audio history, coloring books and more. For immediate first class shipping please remit: Cost within U.S.: $3.00. Cost outside U.S.: $3.00 surface shipping or $5.00 air shipping. Payable in U.S. funds.

Bluestocking Press
P.O. Box 1014 • Dept. PC3 • Placerville • CA • 95667 • USA
Phone orders: 916-621-1123; 800-959-8586 (for MC / Visa orders)
FAX: 916-642-9222